Nothing is more captivating than the sea. Since the beginning of time the expansive bodies of water that cover two-thirds of the earth's surface have intertwined with the history and development of mankind to form a unique and almost miraculous bond.

The vast regions of fresh water in North America known as the Great Lakes share the same captivating qualities as the salt water counterparts into which they flow. Glacial effects, early exploration, shipping channels, recreational activities and abundant fishing, all characterize the important role the Great Lakes have played in history.

Tales of native American encampments, early settlers, violent storms, shipwrecks, and peaceful vistas and winter ice floes, all add to the lore of the Great Lakes. The most tangible reminder of the varied and evolving development of these fresh water seas is the lighthouses. Constructed originally to mark areas of danger to seafarers, lighthouses were eventually built to designate a safe route for passage.

Each lighthouse along the Great Lakes has its own history, its own unique character, its own charm, and its own meaning to those many who venture past either by land or by sea.

This book, this compendium of aerial photographs, is the work of John L. Wagner who has devoted the last six years to capturing the essence of the Great Lakes lighthouses from a perspective never seen before.

John, a skilled pilot and photographer, has worked painstakingly to provide these beautiful lighthouse portraits. Whether it is the presence of huge ice floes in winter, the sparkle of the bright sun off crystal clear water in summer, or the magnificent effect of changing light on the diverse shoreline in fall and spring, John demonstrates his artistic talent in the photographs included in this publication. Each portrait provides a vivid reminder of how captivated we are by the history and national beauty of the Great Lakes.

William Upjohn Parfet

William Upjohn Parfet

Friend, Great Lakes Enthusiast
President of The Upjohn Company

Kalamazoo, Michigan
May 1, 1993

Nothing is more captivating than the sea. Since the beginning of time the expansive bodies of water that cover two-thirds of the earth's surface have intertwined with the history and development of mankind to form a unique and almost miraculous bond.

The vast regions of fresh water in North America known as the Great Lakes share the same captivating qualities as the salt water counterparts into which they flow. Glacial effects, early exploration, shipping channels, recreational activities and abundant fishing, all characterize the important role the Great Lakes have played in history.

Tales of native American encampments, early settlers, violent storms, shipwrecks, and peaceful vistas and winter ice floes, all add to the lore of the Great Lakes. The most tangible reminder of the varied and evolving development of these fresh water seas is the lighthouses. Constructed originally to mark areas of danger to seafarers, lighthouses were eventually built to designate a safe route for passage.

Each lighthouse along the Great Lakes has its own history, its own unique character, its own charm, and its own meaning to those many who venture past either by land or by sea.

This book, this compendium of aerial photographs, is the work of John L. Wagner who has devoted the last six years to capturing the essence of the Great Lakes lighthouses from a perspective never seen before.

John, a skilled pilot and photographer, has worked painstakingly to provide these beautiful lighthouse portraits. Whether it is the presence of huge ice floes in winter, the sparkle of the bright sun off crystal clear water in summer, or the magnificent effect of changing light on the diverse shoreline in fall and spring, John demonstrates his artistic talent in the photographs included in this publication. Each portrait provides a vivid reminder of how captivated we are by the history and natural beauty of the Great Lakes.

William Upjohn Parfet

William Upjohn Parfet

Friend, Great Lakes Enthusiast
President of The Upjohn Company

Kalamazoo, Michigan
May 1, 1993

Waco Classic over the Holland Harbor Light.

"Pancake Ice" from 200' altitude, offshore of South Haven.

Publisher's Cataloging-in-Publication Data
Wagner, John L., 1935-
Michigan Lighthouses, An Aerial Photographic Perspective

p 168: chiefly col. ill.; 28 x 34.5 cm.

Includes index.
ISBN: 1-880311-01-1

1. Lighthouses — Michigan — Pictorial works.
2. Lighthouses — Michigan — History.
3. Lighthouses — Great Lakes — Pictorial works.
I. Title.
VK1024.M5W34 1993
387.155'09774 — dc20 92-96823

Manufactured in the United States of America.
10 9 8 7 6 5 4 3 2 1

Second Printing, June, 1998

This second printing contains fifteen image changes. Technology has
advanced to where separations can now be made directly from color negatives. Three new transparencies replaced images made from "C-prints". Seven
images have been re-scanned from the original negatives. Four remaining
transparencies were re-scanned to improve the quality. And the author's
photo has been updated so persons don't have to ask, "Who's that?"

Lighthouses are for ships! The 1,000 footer *Burns Harbor* downbound off Whitefish Point.

White Shoal
Second Order lens winding mechanism.

This Second Order Fresnel lens from the White Shoal Light is one of only seven on the Great Lakes, five on the U.S. side, four of which were in Michigan waters. The nine-foot diameter lens, now located in the Great Lakes Shipwreck Historical Museum at Whitefish Point, consists of 344 leaded crystal prisms, weighs 3,500 pounds and floats on a mercury bearing surface. The light sequence had a seven and one-half second pause between light beams and was visible for 28 miles. A pendulum that hung 44 feet into the 125 foot tower provided power to rotate the lens and had to be rewound every two hours and eighteen minutes.

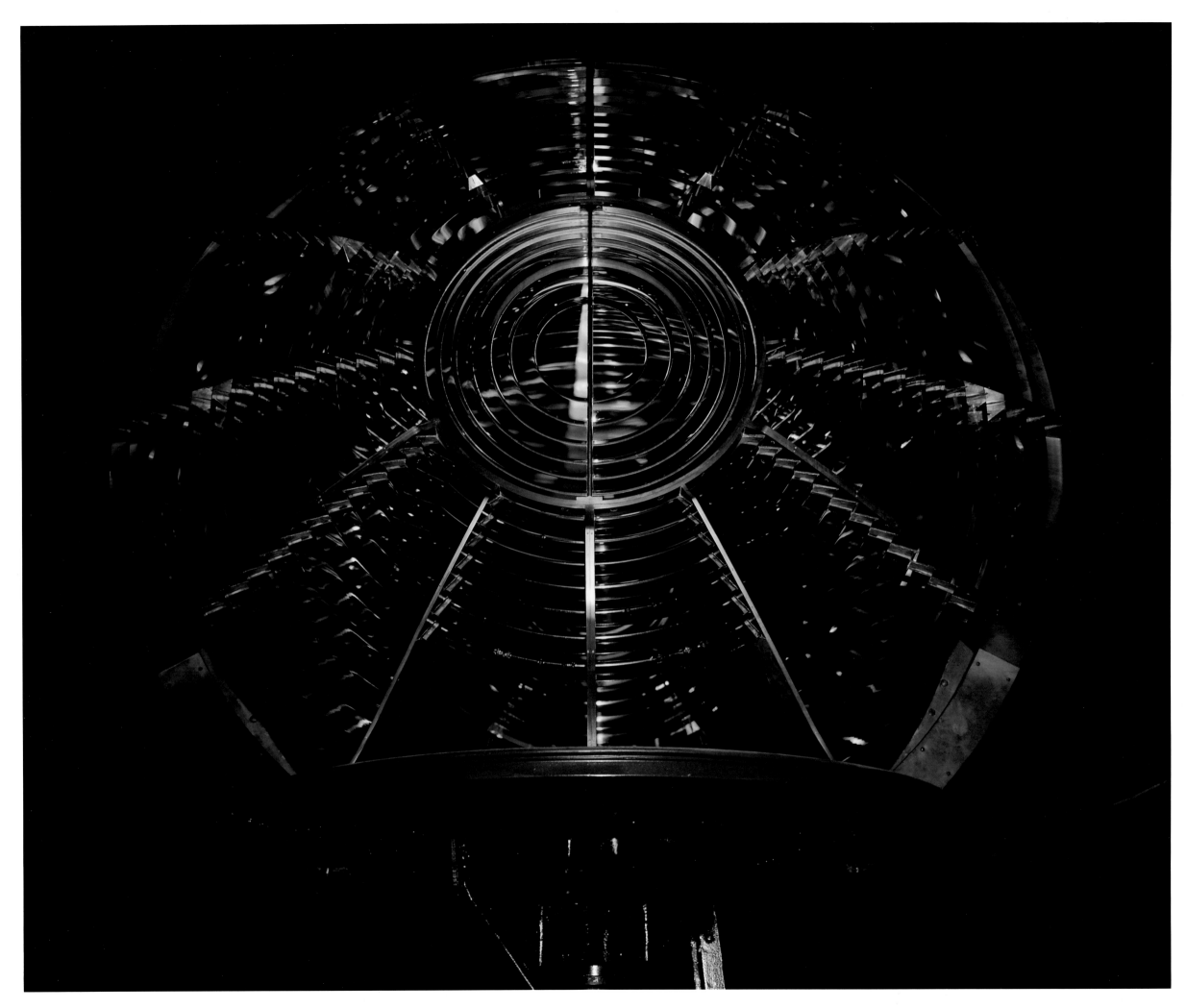

Sleeping Bear Point life saving station.

The Statute of Liberty once served as a lighthouse.

Circa 1964

Lighthouses, A Historical Perspective:

Why have lighthouses captured our imagination? Many of us are interested in the history of lighthouses and some have become supporters of restoration efforts. Others remember relatives who were keepers in the Lighthouse Service. Former Coast Guardsmen, who may have served at a lighthouse or life saving station, retain a sentimental attachment to this meaningful period of their lives. Still others are fascinated by the solitude and hardship that was once a part of such remote duty.

Lighthouses developed in response to our need to explore and conduct commerce. Prior to the recent inventions of the automobile, railroad and airplane, travel has historically been most often by sea. In ancient times, the Phoenicians built bonfires on towering ridges, and later on wooden platforms, to guide ships to port. After weeks or even months of arduous travel, the lighthouse was often the point of arrival or return for the captain, the crew and all the vessel's passengers. Sighting a lighthouse must have triggered emotions transcending all others. The Statue of Liberty once served as a lighthouse.

Transportation is the basis of commerce, and the lighthouse has been fundamental in the growth of the world's transportation systems. The first lighthouse in North America was built at the entrance to Boston Harbor and lit on September 14, 1716. It was destroyed by the British in 1776, but rebuilt seven years later. The early colonies built lighthouses to support their own maritime trade. One of the earliest acts of our U. S. Congress, in 1789, was to establish a federal responsibility for the "necessary support, maintenance and repairs of all lighthouses, beacons, buoys . . . erected, placed, or sunk before the passing of this act, at the entrance of, or within any bay, inlet, harbor or port of the United States, for rendering the navigation thereof easy and safe." In America, the Industrial Revolution depended on the movement by water of raw materials and finished products, something that would have been most difficult and hazardous without our system of lighthouses.

America has few physical links to its past. The Old World has its castles, stone bridges, cathedrals and even whole towns that remain unchanged. The heritage of the lighthouse is important to the country and to Michigan, for it provides a thread of historical continuity in which our relatively young nation may take special pride. Approximately 1,200 lighthouse sites have been established in our history. The dedicated people who manned the lights, the travelers of the lakes, and our whole society benefited from the service they performed. Today, only about 445 lighthouses are still maintained by the United States Coast Guard as navigational aids across the country. The possibility that this link to our past may disappear is an important reason why lighthouses have captured the public imagination. We must record and maintain for future generations such historic landmarks before the opportunity is lost.

Lighthouses Today:

These unique brick, stone and steel structures, that once performed a vital service, have been overtaken by technology. Never again will they be built; their role no longer exists. Today, highly sophisticated electronic navigational systems such as the Inertial Navigational System, Loran C and Global Positioning System, guide vessels of commerce on the seas and in the air as the lighthouse did years ago. Using the same electronic navigational equipment, the Boeing 747 air-freighters have reduced travel time from one continent to another to a fraction of yesteryear.

Notwithstanding these technological advances, the continuation of automated lights proves that visual reference to a landmark is necessary. Carrying with it all the sophistication of modern technology, the tanker, *Exxon Valdez*, struck a shoal a dozen miles off course and created an environmental catastrophe. In Michigan waters, visual markers still provide important references for navigating the several turns in the Saint Marys River between Lakes Superior and Huron, as well as the many other shipping channels and rivers in the system. In Alaska, a navigational light now marks Bligh Reef, the site where 40,000 tons of oil spewed forth into the Gulf of Alaska.

Of major importance in Michigan's development was the ability to transport goods and materials on the Great Lakes. Michigan has over 100 of the approximately 150 lighthouses once established in the western upper Great Lakes, more than any other state in the union. They stand guard and provide reference to over 3,200 miles of shoreline. What would have been the outcome of World War II had it not been for the movement of vast mineral deposits and food products on this extensive network of inland waters? It was the presence of these lighthouses, the men and women of the Lighthouse Service, and after 1939, the United States Coast Guard, that made this transportation system work.

Lighthouses in Michigan are no longer manned. Point Betsie, north of Frankfort, was the last attended light in the state; it was fully automated in 1983. The present day Coast Guard provides only minimal maintenance at many of their properties, and then only the lighting mechanism. They cannot afford, nor are they charged with, maintaining these structures in a historic fashion. The appurtenant buildings have received little attention as evidenced by St. Helena Island, Port Austin Reef and Poverty Island. Some have even been demolished as was Crisp's Point, Skillagalee and Little Sable Point. Other lights (Charity Island, Waugoshance and Fourteen Mile Point) have been decommissioned and abandoned for many years. They have deteriorated seriously — unfortunately, beyond a condition where restoration is practical. The effects of age, the elements, the curious, artifact seekers and vandals have all taken their toll. They are rapidly falling into ruin.

On the other hand, lighthouses that are salvageable such as Port Austin Reef, St. Helena Island, Round Island and Big Sable Point, have

Canadian Navigator, **of ULS International, Inc., Toronto.**

Visual range markers in the Saint Marys River.

Joseph L. Block **of Inland Steel Company, Chicago.**

Waugoshance — *ice on the lighthouse like moss on a tree.*

attracted interested persons or groups to their aid and are being restored. A number of lights have been converted to museums (Sturgeon Point at Harrisville, Beaver Island, Presque Isle, White River, Eagle Harbor and Whitefish Point). Sand Hills, Portage River and Bois Blanc are privately owned. Big Bay Point on Lake Superior has been converted to a Bed and Breakfast. Old Presque Isle is privately owned but is open to the public.

The government's present policy affecting restoration is seriously flawed in the disposal of surplus property. It gives little recognition to groups that have undertaken restoration projects at considerable expense and effort. Currently, they risk loss of the property to another bidder ranking a higher priority. This shortsighted policy discourages the preservation of what remains of our historic lighthouse system.

These various conditions under which the lights now exist, combined with the historical significance of Michigan lighthouses, makes essential an ongoing record of their location, condition and evolution. This book provides a photographic record of these landmarks, many of which are vanishing from the Michigan scene. Such a record will serve as a benchmark of what has been lost and what is — and can be — preserved.

Agawa Canyon
loading at Drummond Island.

graphic designer **William C. Spagnuolo**

To Ron,
Greetings from the author —
May you always have fair winds
and following sea!
Pleasant reading to all ....

Michigan Lighthouses

An Aerial Photographic Perspective

John L Wagner, 2011

pilot/photographer **John L. Wagner**

United States Coast Guard icebreaker *Mackinaw.*

Stewart J. Cort, the first 1,000 footer constructed for the Great Lakes, on its first sail of the season in the Straits of Mackinac.

An Aerial Photographic Perspective:

This photographic series of Michigan lighthouses offers an unique view never seen by most people. Shoal and crib lighthouses, and some island lights, are visible only to boaters — and they don't like to get too close. Even some lights along the shoreline of Lake Superior are not easily accessible.

Winter photography at these locations must be done almost exclusively from the air. During the winter and spring breakup, few vessels can traverse such treacherous, rocky, ice-laden waters, especially when the navigational aids have been retrieved for the season. An aerial perspective vividly portrays the tumultuous force of nature on the waters surrounding Michigan and its lighthouses.

Winter is a very unusual time. I am intrigued by this spectacular and colorful annual event. Winter shots have produced some of the more dramatic photographs in this series. All the hues of light are reflected and displayed in thousands of multi-faceted crystals. Telltale sheets of ice have been pushed and heaved and piled by forces of the dynamic winter weather systems of the northern Great Lakes. The ice floes of spring, with patterns of a jigsaw puzzle, float on the open water surface, drifting in the warming currents towards their extinction. Like snowflakes, no two designs are alike. On a grand scale, they provide the added dimension of interplay between the winds, waves, currents, temperature and light. With transition from night to day and the freezing and thawing of the lake's surface, a constant and fascinating change unfolds. From above I gaze at the various structures in this vast field of ice and water, pondering what caused this infinite variety of patterns and designs.

Huron Island

Middle Island Light Tower.

The aerial perspective portrays a lighthouse in relation to the waters it protects and the geological nature of the surrounding terrain. Lighthouses often seem to take on the character of the topography they represent. The unique and varied geography of Michigan is seen at Huron Island with its bold, barren, rocky-faced cliffs glistening in the sun, white caps breaking at the base, and the keeper's little house of cut stone perched atop. Granite Island and Middle Island Lights blend into a craggy shoreline with sheer drop-offs that disappear into dark blue water.

Aerial photography often brings into perspective the distinguishing characteristics for which the lights were named. An expansive sand beach lies at the water's edge in the winding backdrop of the Sand Point Light photograph. Gull Rock is covered with hundreds of birds. Their droppings have left most of the surface as if brushed with whitewash. A photograph of the Sand Hills Light reveals the paradox of its architecture and sand-blown snowscape, appearing as if a scene from the Arabian Desert, in stark contrast to the frozen backdrop of Lake Superior. And Rock Harbor Light on Isle Royale is truly a "harbor within the rocks." Imagine the ordeals suffered in late fall before the Lighthouse Service or the Coast Guard removed its personnel from that ribbon of stone, just offshore of Isle Royale, known as "Menagerie Island." Its location conjures up thoughts of desolation, hardship and deprivation. Untold tales surely must outnumber those that have been related or recorded.

Lake Superior is the largest (in surface area) freshwater lake in the world. Stannard Rock Lighthouse is located 25 miles and some 12 to 14 minutes flight time from the nearest shore. At first sight I am captivated by its starkness. It is built on a rock shoal projecting upward hundreds of feet from the

Francisco Morazan

U.S.C.G. Mesquite

bottom of Lake Superior, the deepest of the five Great Lakes. Stannard Rock's remoteness has further meaning when we remember that people lived at this inhospitable location for an entire shipping season — thus its nickname "Stranded" Rock. According to legend, there has never been a month when snow has not been recorded at Stannard Rock!

On one occasion, while on a mid-winter photographic flight in upper Lake Michigan, I was skimming along the frozen surface at an altitude well below where I could receive the usual aircraft radio navigational aids. It occurred to me that I had no landmarks to confirm my position, only a vast frozen expanse. At once an image popped into my mind of the mariner in all kinds of wind, wave and weather conditions. The vicious storms of the Great Lakes, the onset of winter with driving snow and reduced visibility, the islands, the hidden rocks and shoals — all threatened his existence if the vessel drifted or were blown off course.

The *Francisco Morazan* ran aground in Lake Michigan on the southern edge of South Manitou Island in a late November 1960 snowstorm. The 246-foot package freighter still lies in fifteen feet of water, only a couple of miles short of, and around the shoreline from, the island's lighthouse. Ironically, the ship came to rest on top of another wreck from a 1903 accident, the *Walter Frost*. Even the United States Coast Guard, in the early morning hours of December 4, 1989, while retrieving a navigational buoy, grounded the cutter *Mesquite* off Keweenaw Point — attesting to the perils of navigation on the Great Lakes. The stranded 180-foot buoy tender was severely pounded against the rocks by the winter's storms. It was damaged beyond repair. In July 1990, the Coast Guard scuttled the *Mesquite* in 100+ feet of water as a monument in the Keweenaw Underwater Preserve. In approximately two hundred years of record-keeping, it is a fair estimate that 4,000 ships have met disaster on the Great Lakes.

1 Rock Of Ages Light	**11A** Copper Harbor Range Lights	**22** Presque Isle Harbor Breakwater Light
2 Isle Royale (Menagerie Island) Light	**12** Gull Rock Light	**23** Marquette Harbor Light
3 Rock Harbor Light	**13** Manitou Island Light	**24** Grand Island Harbor West Channel (Rear Range) Light
4 Passage Island Light	**14** Stannard Rock Light	**25** Munising Range Lights
5 Ontonagon Light	**15** Mendota (Bete Grise) Light	**26** Grand Island East Channel Light
6 Fourteen Mile Point Light	**16** Portage River (Jacobsville) Light	**27** Grand Island North Light
7 Keweenaw Waterway Upper Entrance Light	**17** Portage Lake (Keweenaw) Lower Entrance Light	**28** Au Sable Point Light
8 Sand Hills Light	**18** Sand Point Light	**29** Grand Marais Harbor Range Lights
9 Eagle River Light	**19** Huron Island Light	**30** Crisp's Point Light
10 Eagle Harbor Light	**20** Big Bay Point Light	**31** Whitefish Point Light
11 Copper Harbor Light	**21** Granite Island Light	**32** Point Iroquois Light

Gull Rock ▷

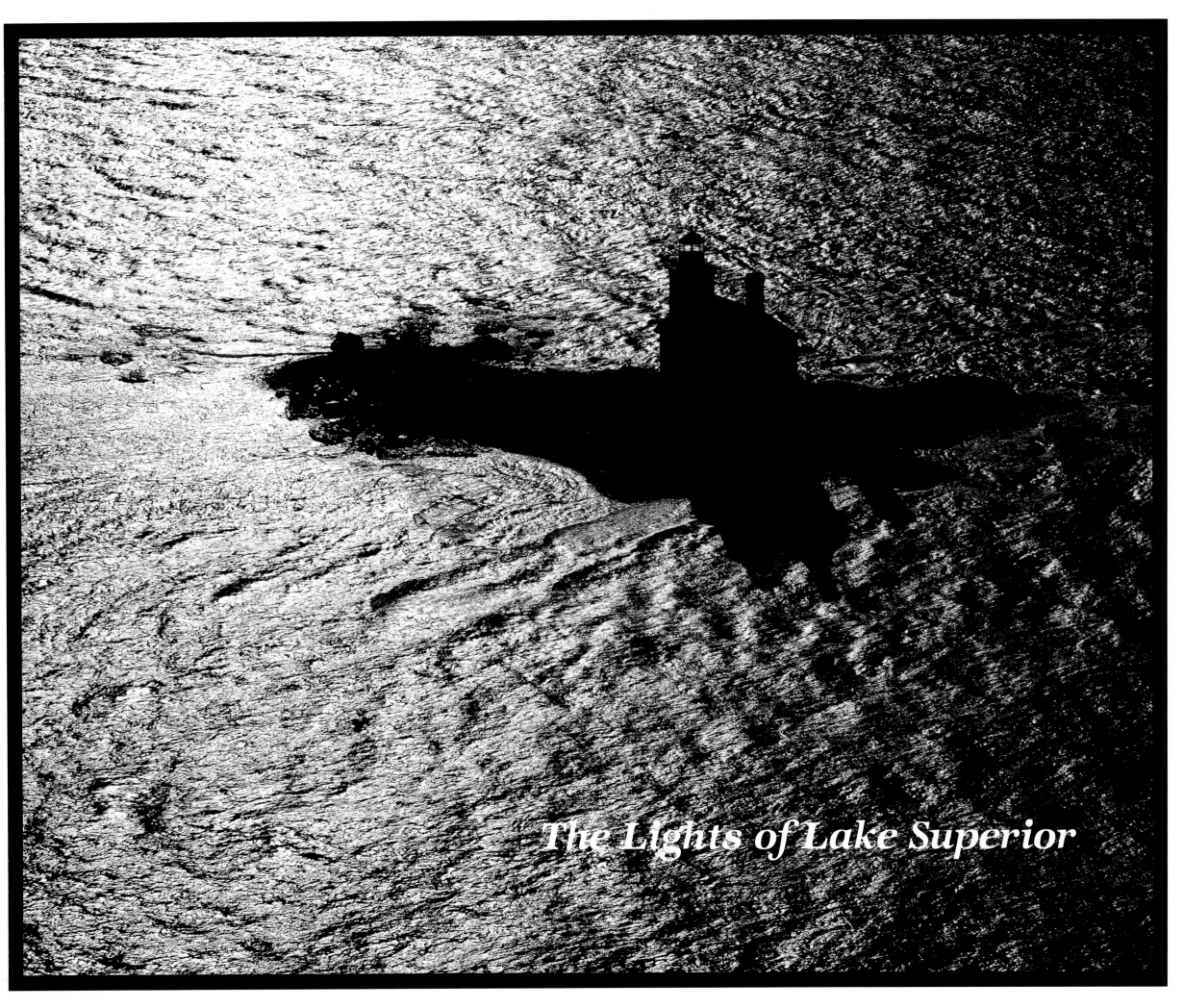

The Lights of Lake Superior

Rock Of Ages Light (1)

Constructed in 1908, Rock of Ages is situated four miles off the southwestern end of Isle Royale in upper Lake Superior. A major engineering feat — blasting off the surface and leveling the rock on which it is located — was required to construct this light. The 130 foot tower once housed a Second Order Fresnel lens that is now on display at Windigo Harbor on Isle Royale. Antennas for the communications, navigation and the remote monitoring system and the solar panels and weather collecting equipment, all make this active light an interesting study of today's automated lighthouses.

Isle Royale (Menagerie Island) Light (2)

Menagerie Island is located three miles offshore at the entrance to Siskiwit Bay, one of the major harbors of refuge on the south side of Isle Royale. Constructed in 1875 of rough red sandstone, this active light casts a lens plane 72 feet above lake level.

Rock Harbor Light (3)

Positioned at the harbor entrance to Isle Royale and constructed in 1855, Rock Harbor Light was an important aid
to shipping when many copper companies were conducting
mining operations on the island. It is now part of Isle Royale
National Park and has received extensive restoration.

Passage Island

Passage Island Light (4)

Constructed in 1882, this light is located four miles off the northeast end of Isle Royale. Passage Island is the northern-most U.S. lighthouse on the Great Lakes and the only Michigan lighthouse with a helicopter landing pad. The buildings at this active light are all the original structures including the keeper's house, fog signal building, light tower and Fresnel lens.

A fog bank at High Island:
When the water is covered, the land mass is open and vice versa.

Logistics:

The logistics of positioning myself to take advantage of the seasons, weather and lighting were often difficult. In August of 1990, I spent three days in the Beaver Island area. One afternoon allowed a good two-hour session photographing the nearby lights of Squaw Island, Beaver Head, White Shoal, Skillagalee and Gray's Reef. Then two days of rain and low ceilings followed. On the third day the weather improved locally, and the ceiling and visibility were picking up in the Ironwood and Duluth areas. But no information was available on weather to the east, along the Lake Superior shoreline. There is an old adage: when the land mass is covered with low visibility and ceiling, the water mass is open, and vice versa. I had found it true in the past, so I decided to test the theory again and headed northwest, outbound from Beaver Island.

The ceiling was three thousand feet with good visibility, but due to a heavy overcast, not really favorable for aerial photography. After updating some photos at Seul Choix and Manistique, I headed southwest to the entrance of Green Bay and the Escanaba region where Poverty Island, St. Martin Island, Minneapolis Shoal and Escanaba Lights are located. Finding no unusual conditions not already photographed, I departed for the western region of the Upper Peninsula. On previous trips I had forgotten or missed the Ontonagon Rear Range Light, which lies tucked inland one-half mile. So the destination was Ontonagon.

Less than twenty minutes out of Escanaba, the weather was again deteriorating. The ceiling was lowering and rain showers were filling the sky and reducing visibility. Conditions were approaching IFR (Instrument Flight Rules). I began to have misgivings. Would I find acceptable weather along Lake Superior or would this sojourn be another futile effort, burning fuel and building C-172 flight time?

Picking my way through five to seven hundred foot ceilings and one to two mile visibility in rain showers, I passed the little grass airport at Sidnaw and picked up the railroad tracks of the Chicago, Milwaukee, St. Paul and Pacific. A railroad bed is built on as level terrain as can be found, so I followed it westbound to the East Branch and on to the Ontonagon River, then northward to Lake Superior.

The surrounding hills were draped with curtains of rain and their tops obscured by clouds — but over the nose of the 172, I could see the deep cut of the Ontonagon as it began its long descent to Lake Superior. About five miles south of the city of Ontonagon, slipping through the river valley almost level with the surrounding terrain, I emerged into a bright, sun-burst sky reflecting off the emerald waters of Lake Superior lying before me. I was elated. The old adage once again held true, and a productive trip along the Upper Peninsula shoreline was at hand.

Ontonagon Light (5)

Located at the harbor entrance to Ontonagon, this light was built in 1867 with an addition in 1890. It served the lumber and copper mining industry of the Upper Peninsula. The building has been used by the Coast Guard Auxiliary. Restoration of the light is in progress with aid from the Bicentennial Lighthouse Fund.

Fourteen Mile Point Light (6)

This once magnificent brick building was severely damaged by a fire, set by vandals in 1984, that destroyed the roof and gutted the interior. Located 14 miles northeast of Ontonagon, the light was constructed in 1894. It has been recently purchased by a private party.

Keweenaw Waterway Upper Entrance Light (7)

Situated at the entrance to the Portage Lake Ship Canal seven miles north northwest of Houghton, the light was constructed in 1950 and remains in operation.

Sand Hills Light (8)

Located on Lake Superior's Keweenaw Peninsula 22 miles northeast of Houghton, Sand Hills was constructed in 1919. The light was manned until 1939, at which time it was automated. Sand Hills was decommissioned in 1954 and is now privately owned.

Eagle River Light (9)

Situated several hundred feet from Lake Superior in the town of Eagle River, the present structure was relocated from the river mouth in 1874.
It served the once important copper mining industry. The lighthouse has been removed from service and is now a private residence.

Eagle Harbor Light (10)

Located on the Keweenaw Peninsula 32 miles northeast of Houghton, the present building was completed in 1871, and a fog signal was added in 1895. Eagle Harbor is an active light and the keeper's dwelling is operated as a public museum by the Keweenaw County Historical Society.

Copper Harbor Range Lights (11-A)

The Copper Harbor Range Lights served an important role, providing guidance into the protection of a safe and sheltered harbor. The rear range light was also the keeper's dwelling and was completed in 1869. The more recent front range light was built in 1964.

Copper Harbor Light (11)

Situated on the east arm of the entrance to Copper Harbor, the present structure was built in 1867. The buildings are now operated by the State of Michigan as a museum and are a part of the Fort Wilkins State Park.

Gull Rock Light (12)

This isolated light was constructed in 1867 on a small island in Lake Superior, located between the tip of the Keweenaw Peninsula and Manitou Island to the east. Before the light was constructed, Gull Rock was a threat to ships passing between the peninsula and the island to reach Keweenaw Bay and western Lake Superior. The deteriorating structure once displayed a Fourth Order Fresnel lens. Gull Rock remains an active light.

Manitou Island Light (13)

Manitou Island is located five miles off the tip of the Keweenaw Peninsula and is the first landfall in the 130-mile distance from Whitefish Point. It was constructed in 1861 on the east end of the three-mile-long island and remains an important and active light. The skeletal steel structure is the same as Whitefish Point and similar in concept to South Fox Island.

A speck on the water . . .

Some ten minutes after I left the shoreline, a speck on the water appeared over the nose of the 172. It steadily increased in size and the underwater formation of a rock shoal, on which the light is built, began to unfold. At last, the tiny, stark, brown stone lighthouse of Stannard Rock stood prominent on the surface of Lake Superior. I saw an array of colors in the blue spectrum of otherwise only black water. The pinnacles of rock provided a backdrop of turquoise and then white, as deep gave way to shallow. The light breeze caused a lapping of waves, occasionally exposing the shoal's surface; a large jagged crack bisected one of the underwater stone formations. It was stirring to see the light tower perched atop a shoal emerging from the depths hundreds of feet beneath — such a diminutive object on this vast watery expanse.

What geological aberration created this bizarre upwelling, twenty-five miles from the nearest shore? When the continents broke apart eons ago, it is logical to think of fragments splitting off into islands and reefs. In some regions volcanic eruptions and coral growths arranged much of the earth's surface. But were not the Great Lakes a product of the ice age?

At the time the light was constructed, Stannard Rock was considered "the most serious danger to navigation in Lake Superior." I knew it was also one of the most remote, difficult and expensive lights to build. Imagine the vessels and mariners who have traversed this area in spring's heavy fog or a blinding blizzard of late fall, uncertain where this menacing formation might lie. We might try to imagine their anxiety for they knew such uncertainty was life-threatening. The lake bottom is strewn with ships and their captains who were uncertain.

Stannard Rock Light (14)

Stannard Rock is located 25 miles from the nearest shore and 45 miles north-northeast of Marquette. Using the equipment developed for Spectacle Reef, the light tower was constructed of pre-cut and fitted granite stone sections, each weighing up to 30 tons, and then transported from a quarry in Ohio. It was completed in 1882 at a cost of $305,000. It once housed a Second Order Fresnel lens, one of four in Michigan waters. It remains an operational light.

Engine Mount Cracks:

During an annual inspection, in June of 1990, two cracks were discovered in the lower left cluster of the engine mount of the Cessna 172. This was characterized by my friendly airplane mechanic as "not a particularly common occurrence." I have contemplated the flight characteristics of a C-172 absent an engine, and they are not very good. Speculating on the direction the engine would take in the process of detaching, while still running, is disconcerting.

These cracks may have occurred in early April 1990 over the Keweenaw Peninsula, at the top of Michigan. I spent a day along the Lake Superior shoreline, flying out to Isle Royale and Stannard Rock, after which I returned to Houghton and remained overnight.

The next morning I headed for the Keweenaw Upper Waterway Entry Light and onward to Eagle River. The velocity of the northwesterly winds, blowing off the spring breakup of Lake Superior, was increasing and colliding with the ascending terrain of the Keweenaw Peninsula. With the sun's uneven heating of the partially snow-covered land mass, the winds and rising air currents seemed to feed on each other with fervent intensity. At Eagle River the spring runoff had swollen the river to almost overflowing. Water draining from the cedar swamps reflected a golden hue on the sun-drenched river's surface as it spewed over the falls and under a little iron and concrete bridge on the roadway. This was a perfect backdrop for the Eagle River Light.

As I set up my pattern at Eagle River, I found the ground speed was wide ranging, increasing dramatically out of the upwind turn and dwindling as I climbed the rising terrain at a height narrowly above the surface. The flight path and altitude were drifting me precariously close to the tree tops, especially dangerous when turning out of the downwind back towards Lake Superior. I quickly exchanged the camera for throttle and added generous power to maintain sufficient lift. One must be alert — a momentary distraction, a misjudgment of timing on the turn or a sudden down-draft posed the real possibility of being smacked against the hillside.

After two or three passes, I prudently abandoned the effort. The flight conditions, fitting the category "severe turbulence," proved too much and required greater concentration flying the airplane. Trying to handle and run the camera under such difficult circumstances was not well advised. I climbed to 3,500 feet where the air mass settled into a horizontal flow. Feeling frustrated and disappointed at having missed such a delightful setting at Eagle River, but happy to be in one piece, I departed the Keweenaw for other locations.

Mendota (Bete Grise) Light (15)

Located on the east side of the Keweenaw Peninsula, 20 miles northeast of Houghton, Bete Grise was constructed in 1895 and is now a private residence.

Portage River (Jacobsville) Light (16)

Constructed in 1870, the lighthouse is now privately owned and located ten miles southeast of Houghton at the entrance to Portage River.

Portage Lake (Keweenaw) Lower Entrance Light (17)

The entry to Portage Lake, eight miles southeast of Houghton, is marked by the Keweenaw Lower Entry Light. It was constructed in 1920 and remains active. This passage has provided safe refuge at times of violent Lake Superior storms. During those occasions as many as 12 to 15 ships have been observed in Portage Lake and the ship canal.

Sand Point Light (18)

Located on Keweenaw Bay one mile northeast of Baraga, Sand Point was constructed in 1878 and is now privately owned.

Huron Island Light (19)

The Huron Islands are located 28 miles southeast of Houghton and four miles offshore. The light, constructed in 1868, continues to be active. As part of the Huron Islands National Wildlife Refuge, the buildings are reportedly slated for future restoration.

Huron Island boat house.

Dick Moehl

The Flying:

My experience is in the field of aviation and aerial photography. Owning an airplane and knowing its mechanical condition permits me a higher degree of confidence for over-water flights, especially in the winter months. The fact that I fly the airplane and take the photographs at the same time eliminates any involvement of another pilot or photographer and thus any question of safety and potential jeopardy to other persons. Other than times of war, some might question the judgment of making long over-water flights in a single engine airplane. This is an added element of risk I have chosen to accept.

Years ago, when flying higher performance, single engine aircraft, a group of us aviators once calculated the glide ratio of a Cessna 210. We determined that at an altitude of 10,000 feet one could glide to either shoreline, crossing upper Lake Michigan between South Manitou and Washington Islands. An old flying compatriot, now a captain with United Airlines, who as a former fireman would dash through burning buildings to save women and children, would turn thin lipped, white knuckled and short of breath whenever we departed a shoreline of one of the "big lakes" in a single engine airplane — even at 10,000 feet. But photographing lighthouses does not allow me to fly at 10,000 feet!

When I began this photographic series, lighthouses along the shoreline were the most logical and convenient to photograph. As time passed, I continued to expand the collection, and flight to the off-shore lights was inevitable. Later, the decision to photograph all the lights, especially when I considered publishing a book, left no alternative. At that juncture, I decided not to contemplate the consequences of a mechanical malfunction. In 8,000 hours of flying, I have never experienced total engine failure in a single engine airplane (although in twin engine aircraft I had one engine fail and one precautionary shut-down due to an oil leak). The consequences of such an event over Lakes Superior or Michigan are obvious. I have never considered the use of flotation or survival equipment. Why linger in Lake Superior in March?

On one occasion, I was departing Stannard Rock, climbing to an altitude of 4,500 feet and heading for Marquette fifty miles to the southwest. I caught myself studying the head winds, altitude and the water's surface condition (choppy), estimating the airplane's glide ratio, and contemplating whether I could swim back to the lighthouse! Such thoughts may signal that the time has come when I have accumulated enough photographs of sites miles offshore. I remind myself, one must be cautious about testing the boundaries of good fortune. No matter how imprudent it may appear, however, such projects become habits of the heart and have a powerful grasp.

Big Bay Point Light (20)

Located 24 miles northwest of Marquette, Big Bay was constructed in 1896. The station was automated in 1941 and sold to private ownership in 1961. Today, the 18-room structure operates as a bed-and-breakfast. The original Third Order Fresnel lens is on display in the separate fog signal building while an automated light remains active.

Granite Island Light (21)

This island of rock is located eleven miles north of Marquette and six miles offshore. Construction in 1868 required blasting of the island's surface to provide a level building site. The light remains active; the original Fourth Order Fresnel lens has been replaced by a beacon atop a steel tower. The cut-stone building stands intact but a section of roof on the west side has opened to the elements. If unchecked, deterioration will accelerate and the task of saving or restoring the structure will become infinitely greater — compounded by the logistics of construction on an island lighthouse in Lake Superior.

Charles E. Wilson off-loading at Presque Isle Harbor.

Presque Isle Harbor Breakwater Light (22)

Positioned at the end of a rugged 2,600 foot limestone breakwater in Presque Isle Harbor, the light, a cylindrical steel tower, was completed in 1941 and continues in operation.

Marquette Harbor Light (23)

Located in Michigan's Upper Peninsula at the north end of
Marquette Bay, the light was constructed in 1866 and reconstructed in 1906.
This active light now serves as a Coast Guard residence.

Grand Island Harbor West Channel (Rear Range) Light (24)

Found three miles west of Munising, this light is also variously known as Bay Furnace, Grand Island Harbor Rear Range, and End of the Road Light. It is part of the Hiawatha National Forest and the U. S. Forest Service eventually plans to allow visitors into the tower. The front light is a new design and is active; the rear range light is inactive but has been refurbished and painted.

Munising Range Lights (25)

These active front and rear range lights were constructed in 1908 to provide guidance in
Munising Bay along the east side of Grand Island. The rear light sits several hundred yards up the hillside
from the front light. The aerial view shows the relationship of the lights, harbor, and city.

Grand Island East Channel Light (26)

Completed in 1868, this picturesque wood-frame building is located at the entrance to Grand Island Harbor. It operated as a lighthouse for about forty-five years. Although some restoration efforts have been undertaken to stabilize the structure, its present condition is cause for a less than optimistic future. Tour boat travelers from Munising to Pictured Rocks pass the light en route.

Grand Island North Light (27)

The height (770 feet mean sea level at the lighthouse — 168 feet above lake level) and prominence of Grand Island in Lake Superior made this early light, completed in 1868, an important landmark. Now inactive, it has been in private hands for several years. The island, owned by the Cleveland Cliffs Iron Company since the turn of the century, was acquired in 1990 by the U.S. Forest Service. It is now a part of the Hiawatha National Forest and designated a National Recreation Area.

Au Sable Point Light (28)

Au Sable Point is located seven miles west of Grand Marais. Constructed in 1874, with an addition in 1909, the structure is 87 feet tall and has a lens focal plane 107 feet above Lake Superior. This active light is part of the Pictured Rocks National Lakeshore. The U.S. Forest Service received $24,000 in funding from the National Historic Preservation Act of 1966 and renovation of the keeper's house has begun. The Grand Sable Dunes, approximately six miles long and one mile wide and comparable in size to Sleeping Bear, lie in the background.

Grand Marais Harbor Range Lights (29)

The harbor entrance to Grand Marais has two active lights established on each end of the breakwater. The 47 foot high inner light was constructed in 1898 and the outer light in 1895.

Crisp's Point Light (30)

Located 12 miles west of Whitefish Point (50 miles northwest of Sault Ste. Marie), this active light was constructed in 1904. The light tower and attached red-roofed brick building are all that remain; the previous fog signal building, keeper's quarters and other outbuildings have been demolished.

Whitefish Point Light (31)

Whitefish Point Light is an active light located 35 miles northwest of Sault Ste. Marie, the important turning point to western Lake Superior. The present steel skeletal structure was completed in 1861. It replaced a stone and mortar building constructed in 1848, the first light on Lake Superior. An identical skeletal light appears on Manitou Island and is similar to South Fox Island. Several dwellings have been and are being restored. Assisted by $58,000 from the Bicentennial Lighthouse Fund, they are part of the Great Lakes Shipwreck Historical Society and Museum complex.

Point Iroquois Light (32) ▷

The British, competing with the French for abundant resources and valuable trade routes in the region, befriended and allied with the powerful Iroquois Nation from the east. The Chippewa were being forced from their homeland to the west. The Chippewa spotted, and with the help of neighboring tribes, defeated an invading war party of 100 Iroquois in 1662. The location has since been known as Point Iroquois — the "place of Iroquois bones."

A stone light tower and a single story light keeper's residence was established in 1858. The present tower and keeper's quarters were built in 1870 and expanded in 1902 and 1944. This inactive light, once displaying a Fourth Order Fresnel lens, was decommissioned in 1962. It was transferred by the Coast Guard to the U. S. Forest Service in 1965 and is now part of the Hiawatha National Forest. Point Iroquois has been placed on the National Register of Historic Places and is operated by the Bay Mills-Brimley Historical Society. Restoration of the buildings began in 1983 and almost $78,000 in aid was received from the Bicentennial Lighthouse Fund.

33 St. Joseph North Pier Inner And Outer Lights

34 South Haven South Pier Light

35 Holland Harbor South Pierhead Light

36 Grand Haven South Pierhead And Inner Pier Lights

37 Muskegon South Pier Light & Harbor

38 White River Light

39 Little Sable Point Light

40 Ludington North Breakwater Light

41 Big Sable Point Light

42 Manistee North Pierhead Light

43 Frankfort North Breakwater Light

44 Point Betsie Light

45 South Manitou Island Light

46 North Manitou Shoal Light

47 Grand Traverse Light

48 Old Mission Point Light

49 Charlevoix Light

50 Little Traverse Light

51 Skillagalee (Ile Aux Galets) Light

52 Gray's Reef Light

53 South Fox Island Light

54 Beaver Island (Beaver Head) Light

55 St. James (Beaver Island) Harbor Light

56 Squaw Island Light

57 Lansing Shoal Light

58 Seul Choix Point Light

59 Manistique Harbor Light

60 Poverty Island Light

61 St. Martin Island Light

62 Menominee Pierhead Light

63 Minneapolis Shoal Light

64 Peninsula Point Light

65 Escanaba (Sand Point) Light

65A Escanaba Crib (Harbor) Light

Skillagalee ▷

The Lights of Lake Michigan

St. Joseph North Pier Inner and Outer Lights (33)

The original lighthouse at this location was constructed in 1832, making it one of the two earliest on Lake Michigan. Located at the outlet of the St. Joseph River, the present lights, which operate as pier range lights, were constructed in 1907 and remain active. The inner light also served as the fog signal building. A catwalk provides access to both lights from the shore.

South Haven South Pier Light (34)

The Harbor entrance to South Haven and the Black River is marked by the South Haven Light, built in 1903. A catwalk, similar to the lights of St. Joseph, Grand Haven and Manistee along the east shore of Lake Michigan, provided access to the light tower during times of severe storms when breaking waves over the pier might otherwise have made the light tower inaccessible.

Holland Harbor South Pierhead Light (35)

The light was constructed in 1907 at the entrance to Holland Harbor and Lake Macatawa (Black Lake) and replaced a wooden structure erected in 1872. The gabled roof reflects the Dutch influence of the area. The steel plated and riveted building, popularly referred to as "Big Red" by the local folks, was automated in 1932 and remains active. The light was abandoned by the Coast Guard in 1970, and the Holland Harbor Lighthouse Historical Commission was organized to preserve and restore this landmark.

Paul Thayer **backing into the harbor at Grand Haven.**

Grand Haven South Pierhead And Inner Pier Lights (36)

Situated at the harbor entrance to the Grand River, this photograph depicts the South Pierhead Light and Inner Light. Constructed in 1875 and reconstructed in 1922, the wood building was sheathed with corrugated iron to prevent deterioration. The catwalk was saved from removal by local funds in the late 1980s. The lights remain operational.

Muskegon South Breakwater Light.

Muskegon South Pier Light & Harbor (37) ▷

Constructed in 1903, the Muskegon Light-house is located at the harbor entrance to Muskegon Lake and River. A second light, a square steel structure, was later constructed at the end of the south breakwater. The Muskegon Coast Guard Station lies in the background.

White River Light (38)

Constructed in 1875, the lighthouse sits on the south shore of the harbor outlet of White Lake, six miles southwest of Whitehall and Montague. No longer an active light, White River is a museum operated by Fruitland Township. The original Fourth Order Fresnel lens is on display.

Little Sable Point Light (39)

Little Sable is located 34 miles north-northwest of Muskegon. Built in 1874, the lens plane is 108 feet above water level. The light was automated in 1954, and the keeper's dwelling was demolished by the Coast Guard. This August photograph, taken shortly after a northwesterly storm, left pools of water on the beach. The late afternoon sun, casting long shadows, creates the image of thousands of pock-marks from footprints in the sand.

Ludington North Breakwater Light (40)

This active light was completed in 1924 and is the survivor of earlier structures. Lake Michigan, the harbor, Pere Marquette Lake and River were an important means of transport for Michigan's then booming lumber industry.

Big Sable Point Light (41)

Big Sable is located eight miles north of Ludington. Originally constructed in 1867, the tower was tuck-pointed in 1880 to preserve its deteriorating brickwork. In 1900, the tower was encased in steel plates and backfilled with concrete again to protect the structure from erosion.

Restoration efforts at this active light have included sandblasting and repainting the light tower and constructing a seawall to protect the light station from the shifting shoreline. The Bicentennial Lighthouse Fund has assisted the Big Sable Lighthouse Keepers Association with these projects.

Manistee North Pierhead Light (42) ▷

Constructed in 1927, this light is located at the outlet of the Manistee River. The elevated 1,200 foot-long catwalk was declared surplus by the Coast Guard and scheduled for demolition in the 1980s. Along with local money, $25,000 from the Bicentennial Lighthouse Fund assisted the city with sandblasting, repair and painting of the forty-eight stanchions and walkway. The Manistee Coast Guard station is visible onshore.

Frankfort North Breakwater Light (43)

Erected in 1932 at the entrance to Frankfort harbor, this 67 foot high pyramidal tower is steel framed and plated and sits on the end of the north breakwater. The Fifth Order Fresnel lens displays a lens focal plane 72 feet above Lake Michigan.

Point Betsie Light (44)

Located six miles north of Frankfort, Point Betsie marks the southern end of the "Manitou Passage." Constructed in 1858, Point Betsie was fully automated in 1983 and was the last manned lighthouse on the east shore of Lake Michigan. It now serves as a Coast Guard residence.

Peter Misener in the Manitou Passage.

Point Betsie Light:

On the day the Point Betsie Light photo was taken, I had flown for over seven hours. The first leg of the flight covered the upper eastern side of the state from the "Thumb" to the Straits of Mackinac. As I headed southwesterly, toward the shoreline of Lake Michigan, the winds were increasing dramatically. Crossing over from Pellston and approaching the Crystal Lake area at an altitude of four or five hundred feet, I was suddenly jarred by turbulence that caused my head to strike the cabin roof and my neck to snap with a memorable crack. By the time I reached the shoreline at Point Betsie, the wind must have been blowing at thirty-five knots plus, and the waves were crashing against the breakwater in a frenzy. In the last light of an October day, the photos had to be taken from the west. That meant flying easterly with a ground speed of over one hundred m.p.h. in bone-rattling turbulence — at an altitude of two hundred feet or less.

The first couple of passes under such conditions help me determine wind velocity, drift and crab angle required. These factors many times leave the wing or its strut, the nose of the airplane, window frame or the wheel fairing in a direct line between the camera and the subject. I must arrive at the right position with the airplane properly configured, a clear view of the subject, and the camera ready. More than once, I've been poised for the shot only to discover that I did not advance the film, pull the dark slide after changing film backs or even turn on the power switch!

When on location, I open and shoot out the front left side window that swings upward. The airflow and "prop wash" hold the window against the wing above. I keep a slight extra margin of airspeed when there is such turbulence. However, at Point Betsie, a sudden down draft would occasionally dump the window closed — often at the very moment I was ready to trip the shutter. A dozen or more passes resulted in only five or six expo-sures. The two or three minute upwind leg, followed by a steep turn to the left, culminated in a brief twenty second run through the downwind pass, when all things must fall quickly into place. To reduce the upwind flight time, I might add power, raise the flaps and re-adjust the trim, or close the window to shut out the noise and cold. But all those actions have to be reversed — undoing, in a few brief moments, all those things that were done — as I am swept back into position over Point Betsie. And this is repeated each time around the circuit.

Flying a photo mission under these conditions, one must be ready to deal with the unexpected. Check the security of the seat latch mechanism or slide it to the aft most position; re-adjust the belt or hunker down deeper in the seat for a better angle, add a touch more engine RPM, shoot in front of the wing strut rather than behind, tolerate the obnoxious stall warning horn, keep an eye out for other aircraft and dodge sea gulls. And don't get pre-occupied with chores inside the cockpit and fly into the water!

I prefer to frame the picture in the camera lens to maximize the negative area, making the timing even more critical. The "window of opportunity" to take the exact shot under these circumstances is frequently only one or two seconds — and seems less.

As hard as I may try to take good care of the camera equipment, such conditions lead to awful abuse with the window slamming closed on the lens and driving it back into my face, or the camera body banging against the window frame or control wheel. Such things are most aggravating at the end of a ten hour flying day. However, when the results return from the photo lab, such frustrations are by then ignored, as they were with Point Betsie. The frothy wave action of a fall gale crashing against the breakwater re-sulted in a memorable photo, and I won't quickly forget that long October day that ended at Point Betsie!

The South Manitou Island ferry, *Mishe Mokwa*, arriving in Leland Harbor.

South Manitou Island Light (45)

South Manitou Island is seven miles northwest of Sleeping Bear Dunes in upper eastern Lake Michigan. The present light tower was constructed in 1858 and rebuilt in 1871 to a height of 100 feet above lake level. The light was abandoned a century later, in 1958. The island and lighthouse are now a part of the Sleeping Bear Dunes National Lakeshore. The Manitou Island Transit provides ferryboat service to the island from the city of Leland.

North Manitou Shoal Light (46)

This early evening March photograph depicts skim ice, broken by narrow areas of open water, reflecting the lighthouse structure. Located in upper Lake Michigan offshore of Sleeping Bear Dunes, South Manitou Shoal is 12 miles west from Leland and in line with South Manitou Island. Constructed in 1935, the steel encased structure is similar to Lansing Shoal Light.

Grand Traverse Light (47)

Located seven miles north of Northport on a stretch of land known as "Cat's Head Point," the lighthouse has been restored and is open to the public as part of the Leelanau State Park. It was built in 1858. The light remains active and a modern beacon has been relocated to a steel tower.

Old Mission Point Light (48)

This wood frame building was constructed in 1870 and is located on Old Mission Point, 20 miles north of Traverse City. It was deactivated as a lighthouse in 1933 and presently operates as the Mission Peninsula Township Park. The caretakers reside in the lighthouse.

Charlevoix Light (49)

One of the more recently built lights, Charlevoix was constructed in 1948 on the south pierhead. This active light has a somewhat unusual open steel base framework, which protects the structure above from wave action and is also an inexpensive method of elevating the light. The Alpena, Grand Marais and Ontonogan Pierhead lights are similar in design.

Little Traverse Light (50)

Located on Harbor Point in Little Traverse Bay adjacent to Harbor Springs, the light was built in 1884 and is privately owned. The location is now marked by a beacon atop a steel tower.

Skillagalee (Ile Aux Galets) Light (51)

Ile Aux Galets or "Island Of Pebbles" is located in upper eastern Lake Michigan. Skillagalee is one of the dozen or more islands comprising the Beaver Island archipelago. It lies 15 miles east of Beaver Island and is the southern-most of four lights marking the upper end of the Manitou Passage. Constructed in 1888, several previous structures have fallen to the ravages of the lake. The keeper's house and fog signal fell to the ravages of the Coast Guard in 1969, when the buildings were demolished.

Gray's Reef Light (52)

Gray's Reef Light, constructed in 1936, is located in upper Lake Michigan 18 miles east northeast of St. James, Beaver Island. Beset by severe weather, the drowning of a workman and the difficult transportation of crews and materials, the engineer and builder, Chester Greiling, nicknamed it "Gray's Grief." The light was manned until 1976, when it was fully automated.

Hanging Around:

A lot of time during this photo series was spent hanging around — waiting for a weather system to clear, for the sun to break from behind the clouds, for a freighter to move into position or a sailboat to tack into a channel. On the occasion of taking Lansing Shoal, the photograph with the ice build-up encircling the crib and flowing water stretching for several hundred yards beyond, I followed the weather patterns over a three-month period, waiting for favorable conditions. But hanging around on the ground is much different than hanging around in the air.

I have occasionally envisioned the "perfect" photograph of an offshore lighthouse with a shaft of sunlight bursting through the overcast, glistening off the floating ice and singularly highlighting the structure. This is more often possible from the ground, where one's only commitment is time, but from the air, time is the pilot's adversary. Occasionally one arrives at such a setting towards the end of a dwindling fuel supply.

The Gray's Reef photograph was such an experience. The photograph was taken after some four and one-half hours of flying, thirty minutes in the vicinity, waiting for the rays of the late afternoon sun to work their way towards the lighthouse. I watched them slowly meandering along the frozen surface some two miles to the southwest. The setting sun had one direction; the winds blowing from another had created layers of shifting clouds, forming a kaleidoscope on the skim ice of Lake Michigan's surface. I too wandered about with only enough power to remain aloft, carefully hoarding the remaining fuel. I studied each little movement of light and guessed at its eventual path.

In the March breakup of Lake Michigan beneath, the floating sheath of ice revealed currents flowing around the lighthouse, forming an irregular pattern of dark blue water interlaced with splotches of wind-blown snow. I had high anticipation of a photograph displaying prismatic colors reflecting off the glistening panorama before me. But the dancing rays of the setting sun never reached Gray's Reef.

The elusive shafts of light, emerging through the alto cumulus filled sky, only skipped off in other directions. The winds aloft were shuffling about the layers of clouds and toying with the little Cessna 172 and the imagination of its pilot.

The notoriously inaccurate fuel gauges, mostly reading too low, were bouncing off empty. This can be disconcerting, even to a long-standing Cessna aircraft owner reaching for maximum range. On these occasions one must be certain that the tanks were "topped off," that fuel has somehow not vented overboard in flight or on the ground. A Cessna parked on uneven ground with full tanks and the left wing low may siphon fuel out the left side vent, and fuel tank sumps may leak. The theft of aviation fuel is not unknown, especially at upstate, out-of-the-way or island airports, where the "local folks" may choose to fuel their vehicles with Avgas.

Fuel gauges, tanks and selectors have long been a nemesis of aviation — and have been the subject of many airworthiness directives (notification of a deficiency requiring corrective action) and lawsuits. Flight time, not the gauges, is always the basis of fuel burn — as long as the precise quantity is known. But even the experienced aviator, having carefully calculated fuel consumption, can find it uncomfortable when the gauges are on empty for an hour or more — especially while over the frigid waters of the Great Lakes.

I finally relented to the inexorable movement of time and my dwindling fuel supply. Before turning to a heading for the Charlevoix airport, I took four or five seemingly futile shots of Gray's Reef, quite convinced I was wasting fuel and film on this rather bleak and gray winter day. When I landed at Charlevoix, I did have the calculated forty-five minute reserve.

A week later I received proofs back from the lab. I was pleasantly surprised to find prints with a warm array of blue and gray pastels which imparted a feeling very unlike the inhospitable conditions that had existed. I also had captured some new and different images for the collection.

The tug *Mari Beth Andrie* and dredge *Clara Andrie* passing White Shoal Light at the top of the Manitou Passage.

Moments of Frustration:

The lighthouse series has been a fascinating and reward-ing project — but not without its frustrations. Turbulence, weather and obscured sunlight, camera malfunctions, as well as tail winds when I'm photographing and a head wind when flying cross country (or so it seems), are some of the adverse conditions.

Turbulence is an exasperating problem. I have flown for thirty-five years, and rough air is just an accepted part of the business, regarded more of an inconvenience than a real concern. In some phases of flight operations, such as hauling freight or "dead heading" with no passengers, one flies with the most favorable winds irrespective of the altitude and turbulence — and learns to live with the discomfort. But when operating a camera at low altitude, turbulence becomes especially troublesome. Periodically, a good bump of rough air would jar the camera in my right hand and trip the shutter, resulting in a strange, abstract and out-of-focus print of some interior aircraft part.

In normal photography one tries to "squeeze" the shutter release button to avoid movement — like the trig-ger on a firearm. After several years I finally analyzed what occurred differently in an airplane. During the slow squeez-ing process, even a minor jolt of air turbulence may trip the shutter — often at the very moment the camera and its long, heavy lens are rotating towards the earth or roof of the airplane. I have concluded a better technique is to cradle the camera in the left hand, sometimes using the fingers as a shock absorber, and briskly snap the shutter release. I am occasionally bemused by photographers lugging around twenty-five pound, three legged tripods. In the air one does not enjoy such benefits.

Once such a jolt of turbulence occurred at the moment I was changing a film back. The camera body locking mech-anism became firmly engaged on the right side but the left side upper hinge pin was misaligned, leaving a one-eighth inch gap between the film back and the camera body. The system sensed the film back was not properly positioned. The dark slide was latched in place and it was not possible to remove the film back by depressing the release button — which rendered the jammed up camera useless. I spent fifteen aggravating minutes, bumping along somewhere in the Manitou Passage, attempting to decipher the camera's "double safety lock mechanism." Pondering my dilemma, I rummaged the airplane interior and found a paper clip which I bent, fashioning it into a tool with a little hook on the end. Probing the various nooks and pins in the narrow slot of the camera back, I finally discovered the right combi-nation to override the release mechanism and remove and reposition the film back — all the while being thrashed about by the invisible surrounding air mass.

South Fox Island Light (53)

South Fox Island is located 25 miles west-northwest of Charlevoix. The original structure was built in 1868 and consisted of the square white brick building with the 30 foot tower atop and the red brick keeper's house to the side. The 60 foot high skeletal steel tower in the foreground was added in 1934. Neither light is operational today.

Facing Page

Beaver Island (Beaver Head) Light (54)

Beaver Island is the largest island in Lake Michigan. Located at the south end, the light was built in 1858 and the keeper's house added in 1866. The structure is presently owned by the Charlevoix Public School District. The antenna, marked with orange balls, serves as a Coast Guard "high level site" communications outlet operated remotely from Sault Ste. Marie. The red brick building, a former fog signal, sets in the foreground at the water's edge.

St. James (Beaver Island) Harbor Light (55)

Constructed in 1870, this active light displays the original Fourth Order Fresnel lens and marks the Beaver Island Harbor entrance.
Only the 41 foot high white-washed brick structure and the boat house of a former life saving station remains. A marker adjacent lists
the names of numerous Beaver Islanders who have been lost at sea.

Squaw Island Light (56)

Located six miles north of Beaver Island, Squaw Island is privately owned. The light has been abandoned since 1928 when it was replaced by Lansing Shoal. This delightfully designed and picturesque red brick keeper's house and octagonal tower suffer from neglect as the elements are on the verge of overtaking and damaging the structure.

Lansing Shoal Light (57)

Lansing Shoal, located 40 miles west of the
Mackinac Bridge and 10 miles north of
Beaver Island, was marked by a "lightship"
(an anchored ship with a beacon) for many
years. The light was constructed in 1928
and automated in 1976. It is now powered
by the solar panel visible just below the
lantern room. Vividly portrayed are the long
winter's effect of strong winds and powerful
waves "ridging" the ice on the lighthouse,
the warming sun and the early March current
flowing from the leeward side.

**Another almost identical ice formation,
from an earlier time, has shifted to
the north of Lansing Shoal.**

Spring Breakup:

On Saturday April 7th, 1990, I flew through the
Manitou Passage and upper Beaver Island area to
survey interesting photographic opportunities. I
found Skillagalee surrounded by ice for many miles.
Further north, the area of Gray's Reef and
Waugoshance was devoid of ice. White Shoal was
encircled by a large ice shelf and Lansing Shoal
was completely free.

The next day, after touring the Upper Peninsula, I retraced the previous day's route, flying at
5,500 feet. From this lofty position (for me), I was
surprised to find a very different condition. Lansing
Shoal was surrounded by ice extending from the
shoreline of Garden Island to a half mile or more
north of the light, a distance of some eight miles.
Skillagalee, which was completely surrounded the
day before, now had only scattered remains. This
immense shift of ice would likely go unnoticed
unless one were looking specifically for such
phenomena.

Where in Lake Michigan might side-by-side ice
floes and molecules separate — one heading south
towards the Chicago River and the other north to
the Straits? This movement over some thirty hours
must have encompassed several hundred square
miles of water — a testament to the action of wind,
waves and currents during spring thaw in the
northern lakes.

The combination tug *Michigan* and petroleum barge *Great Lakes* entering the Straits bound for Cheboygan. The overhead view clearly depicts the system lashing the units together.

Seul Choix Point Light (58) ▷

Seul Choix is French and translates to "only choice." This is the only harbor of refuge along the south shore of the Upper Peninsula 60 miles west of the Mackinac Bridge. Constructed in 1895, a Third Order Fresnel lens once provided a focal plane 80 feet above lake level. This active light is part of the Schoolcraft County Park and is presently equipped with an airways beacon.

Manistique Harbor Light (59)

Built in 1917, the steel tower stands at the end of the east breakwater at the harbor entrance.

Poverty Island Light (60)

Little could those who named the island years ago envision that its dilapidated appearance today would truly reflect its name. Poverty Island is located at the approach to Green Bay from Lake Michigan, 25 miles southeast of Escanaba. Constructed in 1875 at a cost of $21,000, the 70 foot high light tower is connected to the keeper's dwelling by a covered way.

St. Martin Island Light (61)

Located 23 miles southeast of Escanaba at the entrance to Green Bay, this active light, which operated a Fourth Order Fresnel lens, was constructed in 1905. St. Martin Island is described by Dr. Charles Hyde as ". . . the only example of a pure exoskeletal tower on the Great Lakes. The six-sided tower is supported by exterior steel posts which have latticed buttresses that rest on a concrete foundation 17 feet, 6 inches in diameter and 8 feet deep."

Menominee Pierhead Light (62)

Situated at the entrance to the Menominee River from Green Bay, a light has been established at this location since 1877. The present structure was built in 1927 and exhibits a Fourth Order Fresnel lens.

Minneapolis Shoal Light (63)

Minneapolis shoal is located 12 miles southeast of Escanaba at the entrance to Green Bay and was built in 1934. The design is identical to Gray's Reef. Under the U. S. Coast Guard, the offshore lights typically had a five-man crew that worked four weeks on and two off and a four-hour duty shift with eight hours off. The crew took turns cooking, each with his own menu. The lighthouse was supplied every two weeks at the time of personnel rotation. A heavy steel, water-tight door provided a water-level entry to the storage, fog signal and machinery rooms. Two main diesel generators and one back-up provided power to the station. Propane fuel tanks were stored outside the structure, a lesson learned from an explosion at Stannard Rock.

Peninsula Point Light (64)

Located opposite Escanaba on the peninsula separating Big Bay and Little Bay de Noc, Peninsula Point Light was constructed in 1866. The brick tower is all that remains after fire destroyed the keeper's residence in 1959. The light tower is part of the Hiawatha National Forest and is open to the public.

Escanaba (Sand Point) Light (65)

Constructed in 1867, the story-and-a-half brick structure operated until 1939 when it was replaced by the offshore Escanaba Crib Light. The building was converted to a Coast Guard residence and the light tower was removed. In 1985, the Coast Guard declared the building surplus and considered its demolition. The Delta County Historical Society obtained a license to restore and operate it as a public museum. Extensive alterations returned the building to its original design. The cast iron lantern room was moved from Poverty Island and installed on the rebuilt light tower. An original (but inactive) Fourth Order Fresnel lens was located and added to the facility, completing the historical restoration.

Escanaba Crib (Harbor) Light (65-A)

Located one-half mile offshore at the entrance to Little Bay de Noc, this crib light displays the modern compressed air operated fog signal (the white cylinder visible at the structure's top). This automated crib light replaced the Sand Point Lighthouse in 1939.

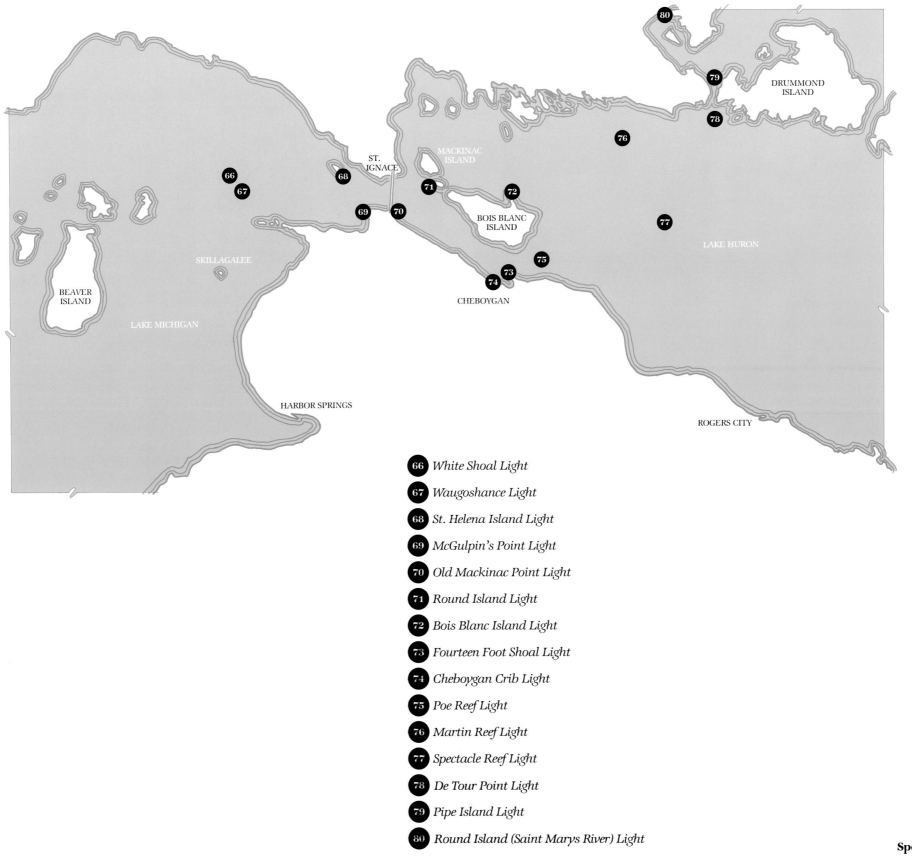

66 *White Shoal Light*

67 *Waugoshance Light*

68 *St. Helena Island Light*

69 *McGulpin's Point Light*

70 *Old Mackinac Point Light*

71 *Round Island Light*

72 *Bois Blanc Island Light*

73 *Fourteen Foot Shoal Light*

74 *Cheboygan Crib Light*

75 *Poe Reef Light*

76 *Martin Reef Light*

77 *Spectacle Reef Light*

78 *De Tour Point Light*

79 *Pipe Island Light*

80 *Round Island (Saint Marys River) Light*

Spectacle Reef ▷

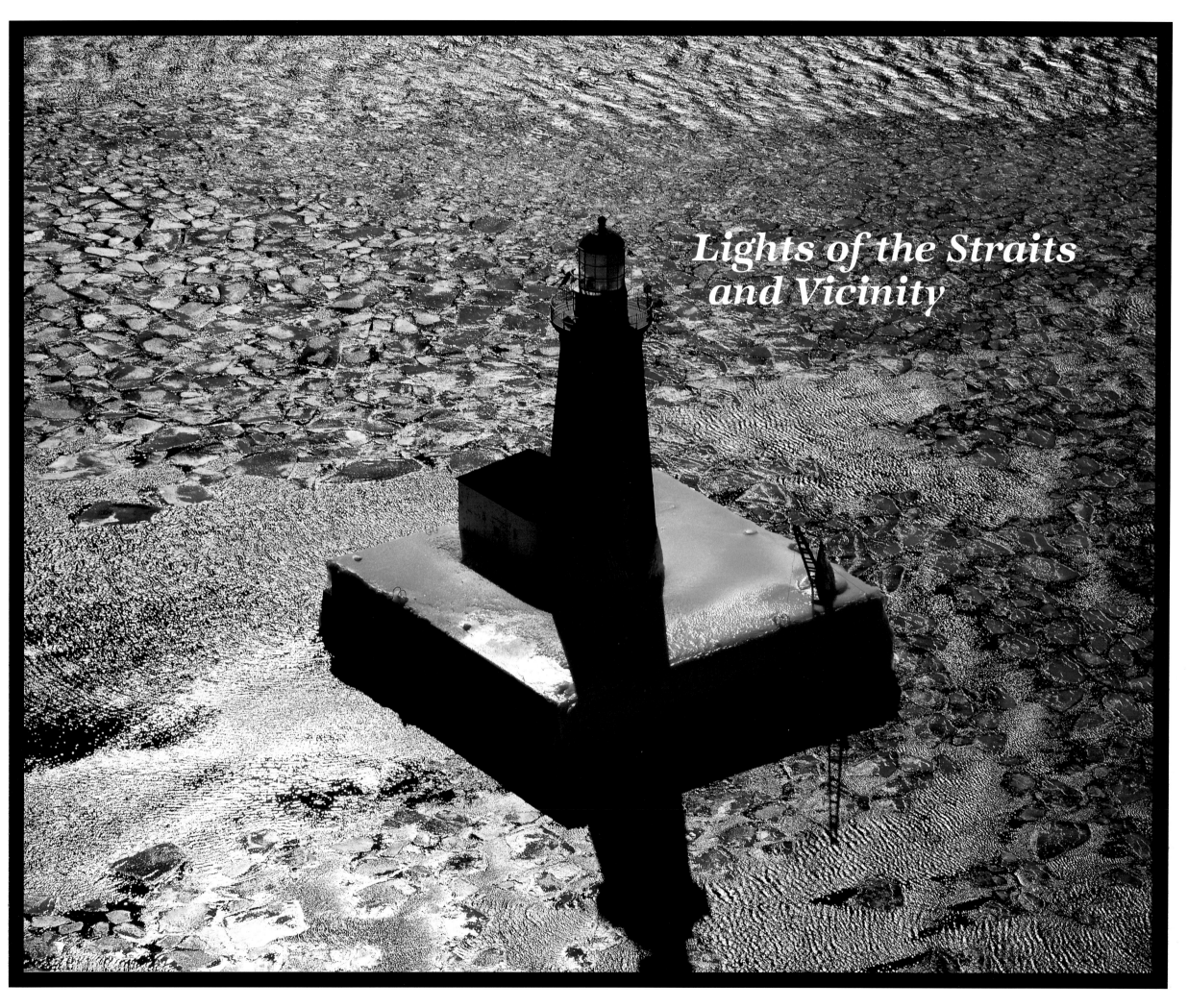

Lights of the Straits and Vicinity

Nature's Dynamic Forces:

The difference in "mean lake elevation" from the Straits of Mackinac to Lake Erie is seven feet. It is twenty-seven feet from Lake Superior to Lake Erie, where the Soo Locks connect and provide transit to ships. But there are no locks in Lake Huron and the connecting St. Clair River, Lake St. Clair and the Detroit River. The rush of water seeking its level is especially evident in the Straits during spring thaw.

The drifting spring ice often backs up in the Straits and extends west several miles into Lake Michigan, as if waiting its turn to pass through or melt. The velocity of the current increases as ice chokes the narrows. To the east, beyond the Mackinac Bridge and into Lake Huron, each surviving ice floe appears from above like particles of matter — and in slow motion they disperse and spew into the expansive outflow of open water.

Once in the Straits, I witnessed the trailing edge of spring's ice sweeping around the Poe Reef Lighthouse, pushed southeast by the energy of winter's meltdown. I was rather casually evaluating the scene, flying around and positioning myself for the best angle, lighting and altitude, cueing in on the ice surrounding the lighthouse. During the first few circuits, a brisk northwesterly wind blew me too close to the structure for a good shot. Suddenly, it occurred to me that the ice pack was sweeping past the lighthouse. Winter's pageant was about to depart.

Disappearing before my eyes was one of several offshore photographs I had anticipated for months and planned into several hours of flying that day. I quickly changed from leisurely circuits to much tighter, gut-sucking turns, adding liberal power and "ham-handing" the yoke rather than making the considerable trim adjustments required for such power changes. I rushed the process and hastily got off a series of shots. I managed, in a few brief moments, to salvage for that year an almost lost opportunity at Poe Reef.

The annual phenomenon of spring thaw on the Great Lakes is a spectacular sight. I think to myself, in a metaphoric sense, Bernoulli's Principle is at work in the currents of the Straits below, as it is on the wings of my plane overhead. The ice floes, as if colossal molecules accelerating through a giant venturi, are akin to the principle providing lift to the wings of the airplane I fly.

United States Coast Guard ice breaking tugs #103 *Mobile Bay* and #104 *Biscayne Bay* in the Straits of Mackinac.

Persistant [sic] winds into a key waterway may result in heavy ridging and rafting of the ice and delay in the opening. On the other hand . . . winds in the opposite direction could flush the ice out into open water areas where it would melt more quickly. The amount of sunshine plays almost as much of a role as temperatures in melting ice . . . so numerous sunny days could deteriorate the ice cover more rapidly than indicated by the forecast dates. . . .
Great Lakes Ice Outlook
National Weather Service Cleveland OH
Mar 7, 1991

Coast Guard ice reports since yesterday noted that coverage in the Straits was down to 90 percent from White Shoal to 5 miles west of the Bridge and a pool of open water extended another mile east toward the Bridge from there. Ice cover was 6-8 inches in the Mackinaw's track . . . but 16-20 inches thick north of the track. The Coast Guard indicated the track was holding well and ice was 'easily penetrable in the track.' . . . high powered ships should be able to navigate any ice areas in the southern lakes without difficulty. In the northern lakes . . . freezing degree days have not reached their peak as yet . . . so ice will continue to form and grow. Hi powered vessels should be able to navigate key waterways without icebreaker assistance by the following dates: . . .
Great Lakes Ice Outlook
National Weather Service Cleveland OH
Mar 7, 1991

Tanker *Enerchem Catalyst* and the U.S.C.G. icebreaker *Mackinaw* in the Strait's ice track.

The aviator's delight and the sailor's dilemma . . .

Returning from a tour of the Upper Peninsula and Isle Royale in late April, I found the conditions in upper Lake Michigan differing widely in a rather narrow geographic range. Some lights were completely surrounded by ice, and at others, all signs of winter were absent. The currents, wind, waves and water depth all have their varying effects on the melting ice and the sculptures that remain.

At White Shoal Light the winter's buildup of ice still lingered, trailing off to the northeast out of the flow of currents, possibly attached to the shallow rock bottom. The floating ice appeared as glistening crystals on the early evening's dark blue water. The air was absolutely dead calm — the aviator's delight and the sailor's dilemma. Not in recent years could I remember such tranquil conditions in the air! During the years of lighthouse photography, I have slowly come to recognize unique photographic opportunities, and this was one. It left a vivid, lasting impression.

At a time when frugality reigned and I thought every shot would be perfect, I splurged from my usual six or seven photos to probably fourteen or fifteen shots, of which five or six were Fugi transparencies. I guess I would never make it as a photographer with The National Geographic Society — they would have exposed a hundred frames at that opportunity!

That picture was taken on negative film, before the idea of a book, and I had depleted my meager supply of Kodachrome. It remains one of the most attractive (and one of my favorite) prints in the lighthouse exhibit.

White Shoal Light (66)

Constructed in 1910, White Shoal is located 20 miles west of the Mackinac Bridge and had a Second Order Fresnel lens, the largest size found on the Great Lakes. The lens has been removed and is now on display at the Great Lakes Shipwreck Historical Museum, Whitefish Point, Michigan. The light was fully automated in 1976.

Waugoshance Light (67)

This picturesque but battered and weatherworn light is located off Waugoshance Point, 19 miles west of Mackinaw City. Originally constructed in 1851 and reconstructed in 1870 and 1883, the light was abandoned in 1912, when it was replaced by White Shoal Light. A metal sheath once encased the light tower (similar to Big Sable Point) to protect brick and mortar from the elements. The shield separated and slipped from the tower in the mid 1980s and now lies approximately 100 feet to the northwest. It is visible from the air, appearing on the lake bottom as a brownish-gray shadow. Waugoshance was used for Naval gunnery practice during World War II. This light has been scheduled for demolition by the Coast Guard for several years. The unique "bird cage" lantern room should be preserved notwithstanding the structure's final disposition.

St. Helena Island Light, March 1988,
from a state of serious deterioration . . .

St. Helena Island Light (68)

During the nineteenth century, St. Helena, a remote island in northern Lake Michigan, was a center of economic activity. Over two hundred residents lived in a village on its north side. There they built boats and salted fish for shipment to New York. St. Helena was the port of last call for those venturing into Lake Michigan and a refueling stop for the wood-burning ships that plied the Great Lakes.

The St. Helena Island Light was completed in 1873 and lies seven miles west of the Mackinac Bridge and two miles off the Gros Cap shore of the upper peninsula. In 1922, the light was automated and the keepers were dismissed. After that, the buildings, except for the tower which to this day is maintained by the Coast Guard as an operating light, deteriorated from lack of maintenance and the effects of weather and vandalism. Today, this lonely light station is all that remains on this now uninhabited island to remind visitors of its illustrious past.

Until a few years ago, St. Helena Island was largely unknown — even to most Michiganians. Then in 1986, the Great Lakes Lighthouse Keepers Association (GLLKA) undertook a project to restore the light station. It was added to the National Register of Historic Places and received a grant of $20,000 from the Bicentennial Lighthouse Fund established by Congress. In 1989, GLLKA involved Boy Scout Troop 4 of Ann Arbor and Troop 200 of Calumet/Larium in the restoration project. The continuing project, now in its fourth year, has already accomplished major renovation of the keeper's dwelling. The exterior, including the roof, windows, shutters and doors have all been replaced or repaired. The security has been increased, greatly reducing vandalism. The oil house and privy have been reconstructed. Other improvements are designed to welcome and inform visitors about the site. Future projects will center on the interior reconstruction.

The project has been the recipient of two national "Take Pride in America" awards and three top "Keep Michigan Beautiful" awards. It also received a 1992 "Hometown Pride" award from the editors of *Midwest Living* magazine. Over sixty articles about the restoration project have been published in newspapers and magazines.

Initially, many people questioned involving young people in the restoration of a historic site. Today, skeptics have become believers. The Scouts have invested over 6,000 hours in the project and still maintain their enthusiasm. GLLKA and the Scouts have demonstrated that young people can make substantial contributions to historic restoration projects by blending adult expertise with the enthusiasm, creativity and energy of youth. The project has provided the Scouts with opportunities for high adventure and advancement — several boys completed the requirements for the rank of Eagle Scout at St. Helena and the project has helped GLLKA achieve its historic restoration and educational goals. St. Helena has been used for conferences to develop educational materials on maritime heritage for elementary, middle and high school students; it has become a laboratory to explore innovative approaches to teaching preservation history. This project provided GLLKA with unparalleled opportunities to mentor a new generation of historic preservationists.

Boy Scouts of Troop 4 during the restoration of St. Helena Island Light.

St. Helena Island Light restoration completed.

McGulpin's Point Light (69)

Located two miles west of Mackinac City, the light was built in 1869 and continued in service until 1906. The Octagonal tower, but no lantern room, remains attached to this now private residence.

Old Mackinac Point Light (70)

This light especially served the car ferries and the Mackinac Island boats between St. Ignace and Mackinaw City for many years. Constructed in 1892, it was removed from service in 1957 after the Mackinac Bridge was completed. It was acquired by the state in 1960. The light is now a maritime museum under the Mackinac Island State Park Commission and has undergone considerable renovation.

Round Island Light (71)

Located on the west end of Round Island opposite the harbor to Mackinac Island, the light was constructed in 1895. Major restoration, rescuing the building from extensive damage, was completed in the mid-1980s with primarily private contributions. The lighthouse has been listed on the National Register of Historic Places by the U.S. Department of Interior and the State Register of Historic Sites.

Bois Blanc Island Light (72)

Bois Blanc Island Light is 15 miles east of the Mackinac Bridge and lies at the tip of Lighthouse Point on the island's north side. The present structure was built in 1868 and operated until 1956. Today, it is privately owned.

Fourteen Foot Shoal Light (73)

Fourteen Foot Shoal was constructed in 1930 at the approach to Cheboygan Harbor. Designed with accommodations for personnel, it was never a manned light and was operated remotely by the crew at Poe Reef.

Cheboygan Crib Light (74)

Once an offshore crib light at the entrance to the Cheboygan River, this tipping light tower with its collapsing foundation was given to the city by the Coast Guard. In 1986, it was relocated onshore. It has since been placed on a foundation on the lake front in the Gordon Turner Park. The range lights, identified by the orange markers, provide guidance into the harbor.

"Once in the Straits, I witnessed the trailing edge of spring's ice sweeping around the Poe Reef Lighthouse, pushed southeast by the energy of winter's meltdown."

Poe Reef Light (75)
Constructed in 1929, Poe Reef was a manned light that also remotely operated nearby Fourteen Foot Shoal Light. Poe Reef is located seven miles northeast of Cheboygan.

Martin Reef Light (76)
Martin Reef was a menace to vessels traversing the area from Lake Superior to Lake Michigan. The light, located 28 miles east of St. Ignace and four miles offshore, was built in 1927 and replaced a lightship that marked the reef for many years. This light once exhibited a Third Order Fresnel lens. It remains active, served by a modern electric Max Lumina Marine Lantern.

Spectacle Reef Light (77)

Spectacle Reef, constructed in 1874, is located in upper Lake Huron approximately 30 miles east of the Mackinac Bridge. It was one of the most difficult and expensive lights to build, requiring over four years and $400,000. The light, built of interlocking pieces of limestone, stands 86 feet high. It contained a Second Order Fresnel lens that has been relocated to the Great Lakes Historical Society in Vermilion, Ohio.

DeTour Reef Light (78)

Located one mile offshore at the entrance to the Saint Marys River, which connects Lakes Huron and Superior, this light remains operational. It was built in 1931 to replace a light located onshore at the town of DeTour. The 63-foot-high steel frame structure, which stands on a 60-foot square concrete pier, brightly displays the last light of day in this late September photograph.

Pipe Island Light (79)

Pipe Island is located four and one half miles north of DeTour in the Saint Marys River and is believed to have been built in approximately 1880 by the Lake Carriers Association. The original 37-foot brick tower, located on the island's south side, once displayed a Fifth Order Fresnel lens. Presently, with an added trellis tower atop, it casts a lens plane 52 feet above lake level.

Round Island in the Saint Marys River

Round Island (Saint Marys River) Light (80)

Constructed in 1892, this was one of two manned lighthouses on the Saint Marys River — buoys and range markers identify the navigational channels. A flight along the river reveals the numerous turns that must be navigated by some ships that exceed three football fields in length. A large portion of this privately owned, nine-acre island serves as a heron rookery.

The Soo Locks at Sault Ste. Marie. ▷

The *Edwin H. Gott* downbound in the Saint Marys River, passing Round Island Light.

81 Forty Mile Point Light

82 Presque Isle Light

83 Old Presque Isle Light

84 Middle Island Light

85 Thunder Bay Island Light

86 Alpena Light

87 Sturgeon Point Light

88 Tawas Point Light

89 Gravelly Shoal Light

90 Charity Island Light

91 Saginaw River Rear Range Light

92 Port Austin Reef Light

93 Pointe Aux Barques Light

94 Harbor Beach Breakwater Light

95 Port Sanilac Light

96 Fort Gratiot Light

97 Lightship Huron

98 Peche Island Rear Range Light

99 St. Clair Flats Old Channel Lights

100 St. Clair Crib Light

101 Windmill Point Light

102 William Livingstone Memorial Light

103 Grosse Ile North Channel Front Range Light

104 Detroit River Light

Gravelly Shoal ▷

Lights of Lake Huron and Southeast

Forty Mile Point Light (81)

Constructed in 1897 and located seven miles northwest of Rogers City, the Forty Mile Point Light remains active.
The building is a private residence but the facility is operated as Presque Isle County Lighthouse Park.

The peninsula of Presque Isle
with its two lighthouses.

Presque Isle Light (82)

The "new" Presque Isle light is located 19 miles north of Alpena. It was built in 1870. One of the taller (109 feet) light towers on the Great Lakes, this active light displays the original Third Order Fresnel lens. It was placed on the National Register of Historic Places in 1983 and is now part of the 100 acre Presque Isle Township Park.

October 1988; the $99,000 reconstruction of the light tower outer wall in progress.

Old Presque Isle Light (83)

Located 17 miles north of Alpena on Lake Huron and constructed in 1840, this lighthouse is privately owned but remains open to the public.

Middle Island

Middle Island Light (84)

Middle Island is located in Lake Huron two miles offshore and 11 miles northeast of Alpena. It was built in 1905 and stands 78 feet tall. Portrayed in this photograph is the entire seven building light station complex on the island's east shore. The rugged lake bottom topography is testament to the need for lighthouses. Solar panels now operate the automated light. The residence, once shared by the keeper and his assistant, is a fine brick structure that has fallen into considerable disrepair. Past restoration efforts have not been successful. It was recently purchased by a private owner. Restoration is now in progress by the Middle Island Lighthouse Keepers Association.

Middle Island light keeper's house.

Fog signal building.

Thunder Bay Island Light (85)

That's why there are lighthouses! was my thought as I approached Thunder Bay Island, very much surprised to see a beached sailboat, some 30 feet or more in length, perched upon the desolate rocks.

The composition of this photograph had to include the sailboat. A very low angular relationship, using the camera in the vertical format with a moderate telephoto lens, was required to capture the lighthouse on the jagged shoreline surrounding the island. It was necessary to fly at an altitude of not more than 50-75 feet.

A southwesterly, quartering tail wind was drifting me into a position where the nose of the airplane kept obscuring the subjects. I needed a more oblique angle in the approach. After two or three circuits, I finally had a better perspective of the relationship of the sailboat to the lighthouse and the shoreline. With every pass, the hundreds of sea gulls sunning on the warm limestone rock took to flight, fleeing the huge red bird invading their territory. After each pass, I quickly set the camera aside and dodged birds. Fortunately, I have found sea gulls to be swift of wing.

The story of the sailboat disaster was told to me by a man from the Harrisville area, who, along with three others, attempted a rescue. Reportedly, the boat had just been purchased in Detroit by a man from San Diego who set sail for Alpena with no charts or insurance — and got as far as Thunder Bay Island. Another quick and expensive lesson in sailing the Great Lakes!

This active light is located ten miles east (offshore) of Alpena; it was originally constructed in 1832 (one of the earliest lights on Lake Huron). A fog signal building was added in 1893.

Fog signal building.

Alpena Light (86)

Constructed in 1914, the Alpena Light marks the entrance to the Thunder Bay River. The Fourth Order Fresnel remains in operation.

Sturgeon Point Light (87)

Located five miles north of Harrisville, Sturgeon Point Light was constructed in 1869 at a cost of $15,000. It was one of four lifesaving stations on Lake Huron and was manned by the Coast Guard until 1941. It has a lens focal plane of 69 feet above the lake. This active light is now operated as a museum by the Alcona Historical Society.

The *George A. Sloan* and *Charles E. Wilson* wintering at Port Calcite.

Winter Flying:

While the winter months provide an aesthetic and dramatic backdrop for the offshore crib and shoal lights, winter flying also entails its own special operating problems. To avoid the considerable cost of hangaring an airplane, I have chosen to tie-down outside year-round. Before each flight, all ice and snow must be removed. In anticipating a flight, I must regularly clean off any accumulation and prevent the thawing and re-freezing of moisture on (or in) important surfaces. Ice inside a prop spinner can cause an imbalance and break the backing plate or throw the spinner from the airplane. Even a thin layer of frost on the wing can disrupt lift and be hazardous. Some airfoils with high wing loading are more susceptible than others. The critical areas are eight to ten inches from the leading edge and three to four feet from the wing tips. The closer an aircraft to its gross takeoff weight, the more critical it is to remove all the ice and frost. My plane, often lightly loaded, is less affected. On the occasion of taking the Lansing Shoal photo, I had maintained a watch of weather conditions over a three-month period, all the while keeping the airplane clean and ready to fly.

Deicing is most often done with a heated solution of water and ethylene glycol sprayed on the aircraft's surface. Some airports and FBOs (Fixed Based Operators) are better equipped than others to handle these procedures. A method of quickly deicing a wing, if heat is available, is to remove a wing inspection panel on each end and pump hot air through, melting ice and frost on the surface. At many locations in the upper regions of the state, hangars, heat and deicing equipment are not available. There, one must brush, scrub and chip off all the night's accumulation. At Northern Airways, in Burlington, Vermont, we lined the office radiator at night with "Indian" back-pack fire extinguishers, warming and ready for the next day's flights. But one invites strange glances in February, lugging a garden sprayer filled with deicing solution, seeking heat and rest in a motel. It is necessary to anticipate such conditions and plan flights accordingly or depart the area before these problems develop.

A reciprocating aircraft engine should be pre-heated in temperatures below 15 to 20 degrees (Fahrenheit). This also calls for heating equipment. Several years ago I switched to a 100% synthetic engine oil. There is good evidence the synthetics offer superior lubrication and operating characteristics, especially in cold weather engine starting. Once in July 1986, an exhaust valve stuck in the guide as the result of "coking" or residue from the lubricating oil on the valve stem and guide. One of the four cylinders went to zero compression. That also encouraged me to change to a synthetic oil at four times the cost. Having a higher flash point with less residue eliminates the problem — at least in theory.

Cessna Service Bulletin: August 14, 1992 . . . Dear Cessna Owner . . . Textron Lycoming has issued mandatory Service Bulletin No. 3888 which requires the inspection of engine exhaust valves and guides. According to Lycoming failure to comply with the provisions of this publication could result in engine failure due to excessive carbon build up between the valve guide and stem resulting in sticking exhaust valves or broken exhaust valves which result from excessive wear (bell-mouthing) of the exhaust valve guide. Compliance is mandatory [sic] shall be accomplished every 400 hours of operation, or earlier if valve sticking is suspected. . . .

One prefers to keep ahead of the solutions!

Another potential problem is carburetor icing, a condition whereby temperature and moisture combine to form ice in the engine's induction (air intake) system. If left unchecked, without the necessary heat applied, it may choke off the air supply and cause the engine to quit. Although it can occur at any time of the year under certain atmospheric conditions, it is of special concern during the winter months when flying at reduced power, especially over the moisture-laden, open water of the lakes. Because of its design, the Lycoming-powered Cessna, like mine, is less susceptible to "carb icing" than those with Continental engines. Nonetheless, one must be alert to such possibilities.

Lengthy flying in the winter months with an open window can also create physical problems. Over a period of time I developed bursitis in my left shoulder which required several weeks of therapy to relieve. I now always wear a windbreaker, even in the summer, over my left arm and shoulder. More recently, I've had to have an upper vertebra periodically rotated back in place, undoubtedly dislocated by the combination of long hours in the air, upper body gyrations and jolts of turbulence with an eight pound camera in my right hand.

Another lesson in aviation:

Despite the iron-clad rule to use time as the measurement of fuel burn, especially when reaching for maximum range, one does not ignore and keeps an eye on the gauges — especially to judge the breadth and duration of the "bounce" off empty. That gut sense once saved me from what might have been a less than desirable ending to a flight.

A student pilot friend, who had just acquired a used Cessna 172, and I were off on a flight up-state. He to gain some cross country experience and I to photograph some lighthouses along the way. He had "topped" the tanks on a preceding night after which we flew two legs of exactly thirty minutes each. A few days later we departed from an airport without fuel service on a flight up the eastern shoreline of the state, visiting the lights from Saginaw River Rear Range to Sturgeon Point and beyond.

After two hours of flying (into what should have been a comfortable three-hour range), I became increasingly suspicious of the motionless fuel gauge needles. With an uncomfortable feeling that not all was correct, especially in a strange airplane, we flew a straight line to the destination airport, Alpena, leaning the mixture control even further.

We learned on landing that precious little fuel remained. I calculated the fuel burn and concluded the Continental 145 engine had consumed over eleven gallons per hour, an extraordinary amount — or fuel was missing. Several days later I discussed with the fledgling pilot the gravity of playing the fuel so close. Only then did I hear the rest of the story.

It had been night when we fueled the high wing airplane and my accomplice could not see the level of gas in the dark filler hole. Perched atop a six foot ladder, he failed to "top it off," not wanting to spill fuel on his new airplane. It is difficult to judge any quantity between full and empty without a calibrated dipstick, so the previous hour of flight lowered the level into an indeterminate range. The shortage of probably three or four gallons per tank equated to another hour of flight. That difference placed us frighteningly close to missing our airport of intended arrival.

Aviation is the survival of the trial-and-error learning process!

Tawas Point Light (88)

Constructed in 1876, Tawas Point remains an active light and Coast Guard billet. It is located on Tawas Point two miles southeast of Tawas City.

Gravelly Shoal Light (89)

Gravelly Shoal marks the entrance to Saginaw Bay between the Thumb and Au Gres. This light was constructed in 1939 and replaced the Charity Island Light five miles to the east. It was the first of the fully automated lights and was never a manned lighthouse. It remains active.

A Coast Guard ice reconnaissance flight over Saginaw [Bay] reported 60 percent coverage of small pancake . . . brash ice over the northern one-half of the bay. On the southern one-half of the bay they reported 40 percent coverage over the western two-thirds and 100 percent fast ice on the eastern one-third. The Coast Guard station at Bay City reported 100 percent coverage of 14 inch ice.
Great Lakes Ice Outlook
National Weather Service Cleveland OH
Feb. 27, 1992

Charity Island Light (90)

Big Charity is a 222 acre island at the entrance to Saginaw Bay, midway between the city of Au Gres and the Thumb. It was named by mariners for its location as being "through the charity of God." The light, being slowly stripped by artifact seekers and vandals, is one of the more badly deteriorated lights of the Great Lakes. Constructed in 1857, it was abandoned in 1939 and replaced by Gravelly Shoal.

Saginaw River
Rear Range Light (91)

Located at the outlet of the Saginaw River, the light was constructed in 1876 and remained in active service until 1962. In 1990, Dow Chemical Company bought the lighthouse, which with the exception of the inlet, was surrounded by their property. A group of Dow employees is seeking ways to restore the structure.

Port Austin Reef Light (92)

Located in Lake Huron two miles offshore at the tip of the Thumb, Port Austin Reef Light was constructed in 1878, modified in 1899 and remains in service. This photograph, taken on a March morning in 1991, depicts the light as restoration nears completion.

Burning the "Tennies":

The Port Austin Reef Lighthouse was abandoned by the Coast Guard in 1953. In 1984, a five-year license was negotiated by Lou Schillinger of Port Austin for the purpose of restoring the light with private funds. The condition of the structure was desperate. The windows of the lighthouse had started to break out as early as 1958. The roof had leaked for years, was mostly rotted and in a partial state of collapse. For over 30 years much of the interior had been exposed to the elements.

More significantly, the lighthouse had been taken over by birds — principally pigeons. It was estimated the flock had grown to as many as five hundred. The remains of that bird population had built up so much over three decades that every step, landing and floor in every room was covered to a depth of eighteen inches with feathers, carcasses, guano and rotted boards. To some that might represent an archeological find, but to the restoration crew it meant three years of shoveling, slipping and fending off flying pigeons.

Restoration of the Port Austin Reef Lighthouse began in 1984. The first summer the crew numbered only three persons. Their equipment consisted of shovels, chain saws, crowbars and hammers. A family pontoon boat soon became a work boat, and then became a barge, hauling people and material over the two-mile trip offshore.

After a period of struggle, it became obvious the first major obstacle was eliminating the birds. One could not walk through the dimly lighted rooms and staircases without dodging and being flapped by escaping pigeons. At one point it was discovered that whenever a pigeon was captured and thrown out a window, it would only circle and return through another. The building had to be bird-proofed and sealed tight, the entire roof rebuilt, the windows replaced or sealed and the nesting stopped before any other work could progress.

Port Austin Reef Light, 1987.

Since the roof over the bathroom was in better condition, it proved to be the best spot for nesting and the raising of young. Clearing the eves, shelves and cupboards required standing on a ladder and reaching blindly behind each rafter, fishing out whatever was there — eggs, squab, nesting material and all. The slanting stairway on the first landing was concealed by a foot and a half of refuse. More than one eager new worker wound up missing a step and sliding to the bottom. It was not a job for the squeamish or weak of heart.

It soon became evident, after a few hours of wading through pigeon debris, that the shoes of the work crew would never again be admitted to anyone's house. In a short time a growing collection of tennis shoes accumulated at the lighthouse.

In 1988, the Port Austin Reef Lighthouse Association was formed with a membership of twenty-three. In the fall of that year, donations were solicited to buy materials to complete the roof. A local construction company donated the labor. Significant things were happening.

At the end of the summer's work in 1989, the lighthouse was declared "pigeon free." Jubilation reigned and a ceremonial bonfire was lit of the rotted timbers and roofing materials. The glow of that evening's blaze faded away to the autumn stars and five years of arduous work was transformed into a completed project. As the night progressed, the tennis shoes that only a devoted lighthouse worker could stand, one by one, were pitched into the fire. The burning of the tennies celebrated another milestone in the restoration of the Port Austin Reef Lighthouse.

In the spring of 1990, interior renovation began. One at-a-time, as money and time permitted, the windows have all been replaced. Plans call for ongoing restoration and making Port Austin Reef a museum replicating the living conditions of an authentic lighthouse. The Coast Guard license has been extended to the year 2020. The lighthouse is now being shown by arranged tours.

The price of restoration? The roofing materials cost $22,000, shingles $5,000, windows $3,000; ladder and crane repair, gloves, paint and miscellaneous expense amounted to $2,000. In addition, gas for the family barge ran $40-50 per weekend. The other intangible cost was the numerous fourteen-hour days many workers spent at the lighthouse. It is estimated a total of over 3,000 hours were spent on the project to date.

The restoration group was a unique blend of personalities and backgrounds: teachers, a lawyer, a medical technician, a tool and die maker, an insurance agent and a jeweler (who performed the invaluable task of rebuilding the crane and winches to lift everything aboard the lighthouse structure). In answer to the question, *How did it all get done?* Lou Schillinger thoughtfully responds, *"Blind perseverance!"*

The Port Austin Reef Lighthouse Association restoration crew.

146

Pointe Aux Barques Light (93)

Located at the northeast tip of the Thumb, ten miles east of Port Austin, this active light is maintained by the Coast Guard and is now operated as "Lighthouse Park" by Huron County.

Harbor Beach Breakwater Light (94)

Constructed in 1885, and still active, it is located at the harbor entrance on a breakwater that is not contiguous to land — access is only by boat. The design is identical to the Detroit River Light. Prior to automation, the Coast Guard personnel rotated each week from the Harbor Beach Life Boat Station, which was responsible for the area from Port Sanilac to Caseville. The station operated a 36 foot wooden, diesel powered, roll-over surf boat that was capable of 20 mph. Harbor Beach was regarded by a former coastguardsman as "good duty and relatively non-eventful, serving mainly the passing freighters with needs such as a sick crewman." The lighthouse operated by a submerged power line from shore and had a stand-by diesel generator. The quarters consisted of a galley and private berths for a crew of three. Radio and television furnished the entertainment and visitors were always welcomed, which usually included a tour of the light tower. A Chief Petty Officer was in charge.

Port Sanilac Light (95)

This nicely maintained, privately owned building at Port Sanilac Harbor, was constructed in 1886. The light, with its Fourth Order Fresnel lens, is maintained by the Coast Guard and remains active.

Fort Gratiot Light

PAGE 150

Fort Gratiot Light (96)

In 1825, Fort Gratiot was the site of the first light station in Michigan and was one of the earliest lighthouses on the Great Lakes. The present structure, built four years later, is located in Port Huron just north of the Blue Water Bridge. It remains an active light and Coast Guard station.

PAGE 151

The 730 foot freighter *Algolake* at Port Huron, passing the Blue Water Bridge and Thomas Edison Inn, upbound into Lake Huron.

Lightship Huron (97)

A lightship, with a beacon atop the lantern mast, was stationed at dangerous reefs and shoals and often preceded lighthouse construction. Early lightships operated fog signals by steam and later on compressed air, as did the Huron. This 97 foot vessel was built in 1921 and had accommodations for a crew of eleven. A tour of duty consisted of eighteen days aboard ship and six days off. A 5,000-pound "mushroom" anchor held it on station. Located on display in 1972 at the Pine Grove Park in Port Huron, it is now open to public admission. The Huron was awarded the prestigious National Historic Landmark designation in 1989.

Peche Island Rear Range Light (98)

A dedication plaque reads: "Built in 1908. Stationed off Peche Island, Ontario, Canada in Lake St. Clair. Restored and dedicated with great pride to Marine City by Michigan National Bank, Port Huron, 8/21/83." The light tower is now located at the Marine City Nautical Park.

St. Clair Flats
Old Channel Lights (99)

Located 10 miles southeast of Mt. Clemens and off Harsens Island, these range lights, also known as the South Channel Lights, were built in 1859 to mark the channel entry into the St. Clair River. The front range light was rebuilt in 1875 after the foundation settled and threatened to topple the tower. It is again badly leaning and the subject of restoration efforts by the "Save Our South Channel Lights" group. In 1990, the lights were placed on the National Register of Historic Places and have received $10,000 from the Bicentennial Lighthouse Fund. Recently, a limestone filled coffer dam was installed to stabilize the structure.

St. Clair Crib Light (100) Constructed in 1941 and located in mid Lake St. Clair, this active light provides navigational guidance between the Detroit River and the St. Clair River.

Tug *Point Carroll* and barge *McAsphalt 401* approaching the St. Clair Crib Light.

Windmill Point Light (101)

Windmill Point is located at the head of the Detroit River from Lake St. Clair. The site of several previous structures, the present tower was built in 1933, and a Sixth Order Fresnel lens, the smallest size made, was installed. The light remains active.

William Livingstone Memorial Light (102)

Located on the northeast end of Belle Isle in the Detroit River, this active light was constructed of white marble in 1929 by private donations as a memorial to William Livingstone, President of the Lake Carriers Association.

Grosse Ile North Channel Front Range Light (103)

Located on the northeast end of the island of Grosse Ile in the Detroit River,
the lighthouse was renovated and is now the property of the Grosse Ile
Historical Society. It was constructed in 1906.

Detroit River Light (104) Constructed in 1885, this active light marks the entrance to the Detroit River from western Lake Erie. The Detroit River and Harbor Beach lights share the same design.

Compelled!

The lantern room of White Shoal Light.

Occasionally I wonder if I have become obsessed with taking pictures in the lighthouse series. When certain lighting, atmospheric or seasonal conditions occur, I have an urge to be out flying and photographing, attempting to capture that unusual image I may have missed but still envision.

With each flight and subsequent review of the photography, I critique my work as if I had taken very poor advantage of the situation. Why did I not notice that the early March afternoon shadow of the light tower at Spectacle Reef looked like a nose supporting spectacles, the underwater gravel shoals after which it was named? I would have taken more photos, focusing on that unusual view from above. Why did I permit the composition of the lighthouse to be obscured by a matching white snow scene, rather then framing it on the narrow band of dark blue water in the backdrop? This or that should have been included or excluded; or the angle, altitude and the lighting was not very satisfactory. In my ongoing quest for better pictures, I consider and anticipate each of these conditions under which I wish to return, searching for and identifying the best month of the year or the ideal time of day for background or lighting. Admittedly, it is easier to view such things from the comforts of an arm chair, than from the left front seat of a C-172.

Some lighthouses pose difficult surroundings. At several of the inactive lights, such as Squaw Island, Fourteen Mile Point or Bois Blanc Island, trees have grown and leave only a narrow glimpse of the structure. Finding the right altitude, lighting, angle and time of year to best depict the subject sometimes takes several attempts. The photographs of Old Mackinac Point and St. Helena Island with the Mackinac Bridge in the backdrop, required a low angle and long lens (to compress the subjects), and a clear day with strong front lighting (in the morning at Old Mackinac Point and late afternoon at St. Helena Island) to highlight the Bridge. These two subjects are only a few miles apart but are best photographed at opposite times of the day. Being in the right place at the right time is helpful.

Some lighthouses have unique characteristics that demand special conditions to best portray some unusual feature of the light or its history. The photo of Waugoshance, taken in the spring of the year, required the right combination of lighting and smooth, clear water, making it possible to see the metal shield, that once encased the tower, lying on the lake bottom. On successive visits each year, the shield appears slightly less visible and may someday be covered with sediment.

Charles Hyde, in his book, The Northern Lights, reports that once Stannard Rock was so encased in twelve feet of ice that "a rescue party of twelve men worked from the eleventh of November through the fifteenth to free the trapped keepers, using steam lines, shovels, and axes to break through." An aerial photograph of that would have been spectacular!

Another lighthouse inviting special conditions was Minneapolis Shoal. The name Minneapolis Shoal is inscribed on the light tower. I wanted to photograph this in the spring of the year with floating ice and the late afternoon sun shining off the name on the lighthouse's northwest side. In three years, I had not been able to arrive at the right time to find these conditions. Unfortunately, when such ideal lighting conditions exist, it is difficult to reach more than a couple of locations at a time. In March of 1992, I finally got that picture. It is found on page 98.

The shoal and crib lights are far more attractive subjects in the winter or during the spring ice break-up. The backdrop often contains infinite patterns of floating ice, blue water, and blowing drifts of snow. I have an unusual winter photograph of Lansing Shoal Light. I remember well the first time I flew by that light during the summer months. I discovered what I could best describe as a block of concrete, topped by glass and covered with the excrement of thousands of sea gulls — not really much to see. This is why so many of the offshore lights have been photographed during the winter and spring months.

To have the interest and the means to fly to these remote locations, to see and photograph such picturesque lighthouse scenes, is an unique and privileged opportunity. I have almost come to assume this as an unfulfilled obligation. Being able to capture these photographs and bring this book to the public, and to watch the faces and hear the joy expressed by those viewing the exhibit, is truly most gratifying.

Photographic Technique:

My goal has been to capture the lighthouses and their landscape as realistically as possible. The photography in the book is true to the subject. No special darkroom techniques are employed in the processing of Kodachrome film and the only manipulations used in the scanning and pre-press work was to match the original transparencies. Varnish was added to sections of the page in the printing process to portray highlights, add a sense of depth to the photo or to protect the surface.

White Shoal's red barber pole striping was repainted in August of 1990. It would have been easy, with today's technology, to digitally retouch the scanned image. But photos of the new paint were re-shot, just as the work was completed. And equally important, images of the original faded paint are part of the record. The photographic variations have been created by the times of the day, seasons of the year and the relationship of the airplane and camera to the terrain on which the subject lies.

Occasionally I am asked what cameras, films, filters and darkroom technique I use and if I have photographed the lights on black and white film. The camera used for almost all the photographs is a 6 x 7cm "medium format," single lens reflex with an image size of 2¼" x 2¾", or about 4.5 times the size of a standard 35mm camera. A collection of five lenses, three film backs and a two-stroke speed grip rounds out the basic equipment list. With the exception of a half-dozen shots, color separations in the book were made from Kodachrome 64, a fine grain transparency film. The prints for the exhibit are made from a color negative film. Both give "first generation" clarity and good detail for each purpose. These are important considerations when the motion of flight and turbulence, and higher shutter speeds and lower ASA film rating are required for sharp resolution. Additionally, evidence indicates exposed Kodachrome has a substantially longer storage life than the dye based transparency films.

I frequently use a moderate telephoto lens (150 and 200mm on the 6 x 7cm camera) that permits me to "stand off" a reasonable distance in the airplane and be as unobtrusive as possible. This slightly "foreshortens" the background and provides an interesting perspective of objects. The only filter used is a UV [0] which reduces the haze induced by ultra violet light. It also protects the lens.

While the larger format camera has the advantages of image size, it also has limitations. The leaf shutter is designed into each lens, rather than a focal plane shutter that is located in the camera body. This adds considerably to the cost of each lens. And the shutter speed is only 1/500 second, an important consideration in eliminating camera motion and blurring of the image. Some current 35mm cameras have shutter speeds of 1/4,000 second. I once tested the 100mm lens and discovered the speed to be 1/263 second (rather than 1/500), which required an immediate overhaul of the lens. As a result, an unknown number of photographs taken at that speed were probably not suitable for reproduction. The 200mm lens, with an actual shutter speed checked by the manufacturer at 1/400 second, was "within an acceptable range." Undoubtedly, cold temperatures of the winter months further impair the shutter's operation.

Additionally, the maximum aperture (f-stop) of the medium format lenses ranges from f/3.5 for the 100mm to f/5.6 for the 250mm lens. This is a couple f-stops short of what contemporary 35mm cameras offer. This, coupled with film speeds of less than 100 ASA, limits low light aerial photography. An expensive addition to one's equipment, especially for aerial work, would be a gyroscopic stabilizer. This offers distinct advantages in reducing movement and blurring, and would permit photographing in lower light conditions. Uncertain, is how a stabilizer would affect my ability to fly and operate a camera at the same time. In any event, the advantages of the larger format far outweigh the disadvantages.

With respect to black and white photographs, I feel the lighthouse series is best portrayed in color. The water and the terrain, the fall and winter seasons, all reflect the nature of Michigan and its colors. Anything less would be an injustice to the subject. Additionally, aerial photography requires a combination of light, film and shutter speeds that does not lend itself to low light, high contrast, exotic photographs often done in black and white using a tripod. Those characteristics found at the location of the light-houses — sandy beaches, rocky shores, craggy lake bottoms, blue water, the natural elements of limestone and copper ore and the subtle tones of dark blue to turquoise found in the winter's ice jam — can only be discovered in the spectrum of color film.

In a sense, such aerial photography is a time when all the components come into play for an instant, capturing the moment on film. That is the essence of still photography, when in the blink of an eye the image may be gone. Unlike the barrage of fleeting images provided by cinema and video, the still photo isolates and preserves that unique combination of events. My photography relies on being there, not on manipulation and laboratory magic. The hours have been spent in the air, not in the darkroom.

**Waterworks Intake Lagoon Light —
a navigational aid in the Detroit River.**

Biographical Background:

The author and pilot/photographer, John L. Wagner, has been flying since 1958 and is a graduate of Western Michigan University and its flight training program. He is the holder of an Airline Transport Pilot Certificate with multi-engine land and single engine land and sea ratings. He has accumulated some 8500 hours of flight time and owns the Cessna 172 from which the Michigan lighthouse photographs were taken.

Mr. Wagner has had a working knowledge of photography since a teenager. He expanded his area of expertise to underwater photography while working as a diver with the Research Division of the Alaskan Bureau of Commercial Fisheries, part of the U.S. Fish and Wildlife Service. He obtained a seaplane rating in Juneau, Alaska, in 1959. Aerial photography has been a natural adjunct to his aviation career, which has involved aircraft sales, Part 135 Air Taxi and corporate flying.

John began the Michigan lighthouse series in 1985 as an incidental photographic interest and continued it with heightened enthusiasm and singleness of purpose in late 1986. In 1989, the concept of a book unfolded. To prepare for publication, further photographic work to include all of Michigan's Lighthouses, using primarily transparency film, was necessary. The first printing occurred in January 1994. A traveling exhibit of aerial photographic enlargements has also been assembled that includes all of Michigan's 100 plus lighthouses.

For almost 25 years, John was employed as an Aviation Safety Specialist with the Michigan Bureau of Aeronautics and was involved with the inspection and licensing of Michigan airports. He edited the Bureau's annual 312-page Michigan Airport Directory for 19 years and served one year as editor of Michigan Aviation, a bimonthly safety and events publication. He retired from the Bureau of Aeronautics in 1997.

Acknowledgments:

To my mother, who every Saturday morning hauled me off, at the age of ten, to Minnie Guhl's art class, and later to the Art Institute in Chicago, and who gave me some perspective on art. She ingrained in me her sense of discipline and knowledge, gained through her work as an instructor of ceramics at the South Bend Art Association and St. Marys College, and in our family's basement workshop. She "loaned" me her Kodak camera on my way to Alaska, which I promptly sold, converting the proceeds to a "state of the art" Exacta.

To my father who thought "aviation would be a thing of the future" and financed my second and third flying payments of $80 each. His feeling that I might discover an eventual use for a pilot's license was perceptive. I have spent most of my adult life working happily in the industry. We did have the chance to share a couple of pleasant occasions along the airways.

My father's ongoing filming of family events meant that a camera was always close at hand. He introduced me to black and white printing as a teenager. He always demonstrated great patience with my learning and confidence in my abilities. For twenty-six years, as an officer with the Michigan State Police, he had traversed the state. At an early age he acquainted me with all its attributes; its seasons, its economy, its roads, and its sheer magnitude. The airplane has allowed me to develop an even keener appreciation for Michigan.

My first flight instructors, Lester "Bill" Zinser and Patrick Schiffer, implanted sufficient philosophy and basic aviation skills in Piper J-5s on skis, to keep me from "doing myself in"—despite my best efforts to do so on more than one occasion. Long time friend, confidant, and fellow aviator, Dr. Arnold Schneider, probably contributed more indirectly than I can measure. And to those many others I have flown with throughout the years—both good and bad, I learned from them all. "Negative data is beneficial to the success of the program," as Dr. Milton Troutman espoused at the Brooks Lake research station, on the Alaska Peninsula.

Particular gratitude goes to Jan Lambright whose photography of the Holland Harbor Light provided the impetus for the aerial series. To her husband, Bill, my old Delta Upsilon fraternity brother, and other friends, who provided the hospitality, good food and drink during the long years it took the idea to materialize.

Thomas L. Jones, Executive Director of the Historical Society of Michigan, first suggested this book and was instrumental in making it happen. He gathered knowledgeable persons with an historical perspective, who in turn became advocates. Tom provided ongoing assistance and inspiration. Many persons offered helpful ideas, information and encouragement. Bill Parfet shared with me a person's most valuable commodity—time; he challenged and expanded my thoughts and lent assurance at key times. George Weeks was always available and a steady voice when ideas were needed or problems were to be solved. And my thanks to former governor, William G. Milliken, for his words of tribute to our great state of Michigan.

Dick Moehl, president of the Great Lakes Lighthouse Keepers Association (GLLKA), contributed ideas and encouragement, and has been perhaps my greatest friend and ally. His decision to involve the Boy Scouts in the restoration of the St. Helena Island Light speaks most highly of a commitment to teach and to instill a tradition of history in today's youth. Leo and Sue Kushel offered endless encouragement and occasional historical data from their vast lighthouse files. They also are tireless followers and supporters of restoration efforts.

Others were John Logie, Warren Hecker and Margery Teggelaar of Grand Rapids; Mike and Darla Van Hoey; Lou Schillinger and the folks of The Port Austin Reef Lighthouse Association. Former Coast Guardsmen Jim Hoffman, Dick O'Neal and Roy Boudreau all offered anecdotes and enticing commentary on life at a light station. Les Kirby freely shared his expertise. Ken Schaschl, my friend and computer guru, often bailed me out and kept me up to speed on the latest hardware and programs.

A network of assistance unfolded from Jim Barrett and the Michigan Chamber of Commerce. Important initial contacts from persons who saw my lighthouse photographs led eventually to this publication. I might add that no financial aid came from any source—either Bronica or Kodak (they were invited) nor were any grant, foundation or public moneys used in this project. Good old fashioned enthusiasm and entrepreneurship made it happen.

Graphic designer, Bill Spagnuolo brought to the project an unique blend of ideas, design, printing, typesetting and color separation experience and skills. His varied talents and attention to detail were instrumental in compiling this collection in book form.

Last, and most importantly, Dr. Clara Lee Moodie, and also Dr. Peter Fries and Nancy Fries, of Central Michigan University, were essential to the project. Their writing assistance helped me convey thoughts with clarity and meaning. Their inspiration throughout the project prevented its languishing.

And to those whom I might have missed or ignored, I grant you the personal satisfaction of knowing that "he couldn't have done it without me!"

Credits:

Design: Spagnuolo Design, William C. Spagnuolo
Pre-press: Electronic Page Layout, Macintosh
    Digital color scanning: Hell 3000 system
    Digital color proofing: Iris
    Film recording: 400 line screen; Scitex Dolev 800
Printing: Superior Colour Graphics, Kalamazoo, Michigan
    High Definition Color Printing at 400 line screen water-
    less on a Komori Lithrone 640 with coating tower.
    Printed four color process with fifth color type and sixth
    color special varnish treatment.
Type Font: Zaph International (ITC)
Paper: Dust Cover, McCoy 100# Text Gloss
    Text: McCoy 100# Silk
        Manufacturer, Potlach Paper Company,
        Cloquet, Minnesota
    End Leaf: Valley Forge Parchment, 65# Cover, Script Blue
        Manufacturer: Fox River Paper Company,
        Appleton, Wisconsin
        Supplier: Quimby-Walstrom Paper Company,
        Grand Rapids, Michigan
    Fly Page: Glama Natural Clear, 29#
        Manufacturer: Schoellershammer Paper Mill,
        Duren, Germany
        Supplier, Central Michigan Paper Company,
        Grand Rapids, Michigan
Bindery: Nicholstone Bindery Companies, Inc., Nashville,
    Tennessee
Camera: Bronica GS-1, 6x7 cm
Film: Kodak Kodachrome 64
Map Drawings: Fred Bork
Financing: Old Kent Bank and Trust Company,
    Grand Rapids, Michigan
Classic Aircraft Company: Lansing, Michigan for providing
    the Waco biplane

Much of the data and historical information referred to is
based upon Dr. Charles K. Hyde's *The Northern Lights,
Lighthouses of The Upper Great Lakes,* (available from the
Wayne State University Press, Phone: 800-978-7323). I recognize and appreciate this fine composition and the photography of John and Ann Mahan. My effort was made immensely
easier as the result of their work.

Great Lakes Lighthouse Keepers Association (GLLKA)
Persons seeking additional information or wishing to become
actively involved in lighthouse restoration or historical activi-
ties are invited to join the Great Lakes Lighthouse Keepers
Association (GLLKA), c/o Henry Ford Estate, 4901 Evergreen
Road, Dearborn, Michigan, 48128; Phone: 313-436-9150,
Fax: 313-436-9143.

Historical Society of Michigan
The Historical Society of Michigan recognized lighthouses as a
crucial part of Michigan history. I offer a special tribute in
memory of Thomas L. Jones, former Executive Director, for
his important support in the creation of this work. Persons
wishing information on Society activities or membership may
contact the organization at: 2117 Washtenaw Avenue,
Ann Arbor, Michigan, 48104-4599; Phone: 734-769-1828,
Fax: 734-769-4267.

**Muskegon Coast Guard Station
and South Pier Light**

Additional Reading:

Carse, Robert, Keepers of the Lights, A History of American Lighthouses, 176 pages, illustrated, maps. Scribner, New York, NY, ©1969.

Cesar, Pete, Let There be Light, 102 pages, illustrated, maps. Ocean & Great Lakes Marine Press, Green Bay, WI, ©1984.

Hyde, Charles, K., The Northern Lights, Lighthouses of The Upper Great Lakes, 208 pages, photographs, illustrated, maps. TwoPeninsula Press, Michigan Natural Resources Magazine, Box 30034, Lansing, MI 48909, ©1986.

Kuschel, Leo and Sue, Lighthouse Locator Guide. A collection of 366 lights of the five Great Lakes including Canada, contained on two 23" x 35" charts. Published by Historical Society of Michigan, 2117 Washtenaw Avenue, Ann Arbor, MI 48104 and Great Lakes Lighthouse Keepers Association, ©1991.

Law, William H., Among the Lighthouses of the Great Lakes. Detroit, MI, ©1908.

Manse, Thomas J. and Le Lievre, Roger, Know Your Ships, The Seaway Issue. 121 pages, photographs, cross-reference index, Marine Publishing Co., PO Box 68, Sault Ste. Marie, MI 49783, ©1992.

Noble, Dennis L., Sentinels of the Rocks: from "Graveyard Coast" to National Lakeshore. 61 pages, illustrated. Northern Michigan Press, Marquette, MI, ©1979.

Penrose, Bill T. & Laurie, A Traveler's Guide to 116 Michigan Lighthouses. 111 pages, photographs, illustrated. Friede Publications, 2339 Venezia Drive, Davison, MI 48423, ©1992.

Splake, T. Kilgore, Superior Land Lights, 45 pages, illustrated. Angst Productions, Battle Creek, MI. ©1984.

Swayze, David D., SHIPWRECK! A Comprehensive Directory of Over 3,700 Shipwrecks on the Great Lakes. 260 pages, Harbor House Publishers, Inc., 221 Water Street, Boyne City, MI 49712, ©1992.

U.S. Lighthouses: A Bicentennial, 1789-1989. United States Coast Guard.

Witney, Dudley, The Lighthouse. 256 pages, illustrated. Arch Cape Press, a division of Dilithum Press, Ltd., 225 Park Avenue South, New York, NY, 10003, ©1975.

The abandoned U.S. Coast Guard Life Saving Station at Harbor Beach — *another decaying relic of the past.*

Alphabetical Index of the Lights:

Two Sisters at Sunset
St. Clair Flats Old Channel Lights